paige tate & co.

Copyright © 2021 Nikki Boyd

Published by Paige Tate & Co.
Paige Tate & Co. is an imprint of Blue Star Press
PO Box 8835, Bend, OR 97708
contact@bluestarpress.com
www.bluestarpress.com

Design by Chris Ramirez
Photography by Katie Lybrand of Katie Charlotte Photography
Photographs on pages 17, 71, and 107 from Creative Market under an extended license.

ISBN 9781950968251

Printed in Mexico

10 9 8 7 6 5 4 3 2 1

BEAUTIFULLY ORGANIZED

at work

BRING ORDER AND JOY TO
YOUR WORK LIFE SO YOU CAN
STAY CALM, RELIEVE STRESS,
AND GET MORE DONE EACH DAY

NIKKI BOYD

CREATOR OF ATHOMEWITHNIKKI.COM

TABLE OF CONTENTS

INTRODUCTION

Before I owned my professional organizing business, I worked at a number of different companies. One position in particular really stands out to me.

My husband's job in the United States Air Force had just moved our family to a new area of the country, and I was eager to meet people and begin building our life in this place. Thankfully, I quickly landed a job that would allow me to do just that. I was excited to get started.

On my first day of work, I set my alarm extra early to make sure I got to the office on time. (I had even done a test run of my commute the week before to make sure I knew how much time it would take me to get there in the morning traffic.) I arrived at the office 10 minutes before my scheduled start time and entered the elevator with pep in my step. That's when I noticed a strange smell in the air, one that screamed, "This place needs housekeeping help!" I shivered but tried to ignore it and stay positive.

As I got off the elevator, I approached the receptionist and introduced myself with a friendly, "Hello!" She didn't even look up to acknowledge me. After I had made several attempts to grab her attention and announce that this was my first day, she finally looked up and told me to have a seat and wait for my manager.

My new manager rushed out in a disheveled state a few minutes later. Her first words to me were, "You are 10 minutes early!" I could tell she didn't mean that in a good way. Red flags were starting to pop up all over the place.

My manager escorted me to my work area: a large room filled with cubicles. As I arrived at my dusty cubicle, I noticed that the previous occupant had forgotten to take their things. I spent the rest of my first day sorting through their items and dealing with the clutter that had been left behind.

As I drove home that evening, I was exhausted, disappointed, and lonely. Thankfully, my spirits were lifted when I arrived at my clean, organized, peaceful house. I immediately took a shower to try to wash the day away, but my mind was still reeling. I didn't understand how my new colleagues could choose to work in such a dysfunctional and disorganized environment every day. The effects it was having on them were obvious: The managers and team members were miserable and rude, and the office itself was dirty and depressing.

After my shower I felt rejuvenated and determined to change my work environment. I immediately started "shopping" my home for a lamp, coordinated office accessories, and some much-needed cleaning supplies.

The next day, I arrived at work and began transforming my workspace into a well-organized cubicle. This quickly sparked conversations among my teammates, who just the day before had treated me as though I were invisible.

I plugged in my lamp and turned it on. The light was like rays of sunshine beaming out from my cubicle space, creating a mood that was inviting and motivating yet professional. I decorated my desk with my coordinated accessories, breathed a sigh of relief, and began my day. I had created a space that was clean and energized—just what I needed to be able to focus on doing my best work.

A few days later, the director of my department walked by my cubicle, and I caught a look of joy on his face. My simple actions had been noticed. Over the next few weeks, my coworkers also felt motivated to bring in their own lamps and accessories to organize their areas. Although there was still much work to be done to transform that space into a beautifully organized office, I noticed several cubicles radiating with light and blooming with beauty in the weeks that followed.

Over the years, experiences like these have taught me that one's happiness at work is as important as one's happiness at home. Why? Because both impact your emotional well-being as well as that of your family. After writing my first book, *Beautifully Organized: A Guide to Function and Style in Your Home*, I knew

I wanted to create a book that would help bring beauty and order to the workplace as well.

Disorganization at work leads to confusion and stress for far too many people. For the past few years, many of my professional organizing clients have come to me overwhelmed and frustrated that they couldn't make their workspaces *work* for them: Clutter and a lack of order got in the way of their being able to be happy and productive. I work with my clients to identify their top stressors and make a few simple changes to their workspaces and work life. Once we've done that, they find themselves feeling a huge sense of relief. They realize that while their workdays may be busy and stressful at times, the space where they complete their work doesn't have to be.

These days, work looks different for so many of us. Some people report to an office each day; others juggle working from home with other daily tasks. Some may be retired, homeschooling their kids, or running their own businesses. But no matter the situation, work is something that commands a lot of our attention and energy, which is why organization is so essential.

In addition to the work I do with my clients, I also share tips on my YouTube channel At Work with Nikki (AtWorkWithNikki), and now I'll share my advice with you in this book. In *Beautifully Organized at Work*, you will learn how to create your own beautifully organized work environment that will help you lessen stress, work more efficiently, and leave your job feeling motivated and excited to return the next day. Let's get started!

CHAPTER ONE

WHERE TO BEGIN

Before you set out to create a beautifully organized workspace, I believe it is important to first get in the right mindset about creating and maintaining that kind of environment.

Organizing your workspace is about more than tidying up your desk or decluttering your file cabinet. It is about creating an environment where you can focus on the work that matters most to you. The goal is to create a space where you can actually enjoy work and end each day feeling like you were able to accomplish what you wanted.

Over the years, I have worked in a variety of workspaces: in a cubicle, in shared spaces, in private offices, at home, and even on the go in my car. I've also worked for myself and with teams large and small. Throughout this book, I'll cover how to work successfully in each of these situations. Regardless of where you work, though, the only way you will get organized and stay organized is if you adopt a positive attitude and determined approach to the task ahead.

MOTIVATE YOURSELF

Start by defining how you want to feel at work. "Home is where the heart is," as the saying goes, but work is where we spend most of our time. Unfortunately, when many of us think of work, happy, joyful, and exciting aren't the first words that come to mind. For most people, the dictionary definition of work—an activity involving mental or physical effort done in order to achieve a purpose or result—is the most accurate one. But if you want the place where you invest so much of your time and energy to be more enjoyable, then one of the first steps is to define how you want to feel in that space each day.

◄ ASK YOURSELF ►

How do I want to feel at work? (Grab a journal, a notepad, or your smartphone, and write down a few words that describe what you desire. Below are a few examples to inspire you.)

CALM   FOCUSED   CENTERED

MOTIVATED   ENERGIZED   INSPIRED   CREATIVE

CHALLENGED   INNOVATIVE   CONFIDENT

AMBITIOUS   DRIVEN   ORGANIZED   HARDWORKING

COLLABORATIVE   HAPPY   JOYFUL

CHEERFUL   COMFORTABLE   RELAXED   AT EASE

IDENTIFY YOUR TOP STRESSORS AND GOALS

Now that you have identified how you want to feel at work, it's time to ask yourself what stressors and barriers are getting in your way. Whenever I start working with a client, I always try to identify their top sources of stress first. Is it a disheveled desk? An overflowing e-mail inbox? A lack of balance and boundaries between work and home? As you embark on this journey, I want you to reflect on why reimagining your workspace has become a priority for you.

◄ *ASK YOURSELF* ►

- What is causing me the most stress at work and preventing me from feeling the way I want to feel?

- Where could my workspace use the most help?

- In what ways is my work life not working for me?

Once you have identified your top stressors at work, reframe them into mission-driven goals that can help you take action toward reducing that stress. Here are some examples.

STRESSOR		GOAL
I am stressed out about my disheveled desk.	►	I want to create a clean workspace where everything has its place.
My file cabinet is cluttered and out of control.	►	I want to focus on organizing my files so I can quickly find important information.
Rushing into work each morning after a long commute sets a negative tone for my day.	►	I want to learn how to take a moment to calm myself before I sit down at my desk.

REDEFINE THE WORD *WORK*

As a professional organizer, almost every home kitchen I encounter has a "junk drawer." In most cases, the junk drawer represents its name very well: It's the messy, cluttered, stressful space in the kitchen. Even the term establishes that the space is likely disorganized and filled with unimportant items. That is why I recommend you shift your focus and instead think of it as a "utility drawer."

Reframing your thoughts can help you view a space as beneficial and useful, and I want you to do the same for your workspace. Instead of just thinking of it as the place where you do your job, what if you thought about it as your "work home"? Adding that one word helps bring a dose of positivity and warmth to your approach to work and the environment you are hoping to create. If that phrase isn't your style, you can come up with your own vision for what you want your workspace to represent in your life.

◄ ASK YOURSELF ►

- When I close my eyes and envision my ideal workspace, what does it look like?

- How can I make my workspace reflect my personality and needs?

- Are there elements from my home life that I could use as inspiration for my workspace? How can I make my office feel homier?

TURN WORK GUILT INTO WORK GRATITUDE

You have most likely had a job at some point in your career that you didn't like, one that you complained about every day. This may even be the case for you now. If you are worried that it will be difficult to stay motivated and organized, it might be because just the thought of work stresses you out. On the days when you lie in bed, struggling to find the energy to start your day, then I recommend trying to think about someone who wishes they had your job—or any job, for that matter. Think about the days in college when you dreamed of having your current career and how hard you've worked to get to this place in your life.

On days when I'm feeling really unmotivated, I often guilt myself by thinking about someone who wishes they had two working legs to get up and go to work like I am blessed and able to do, or I think about a person who wishes they could see the beautiful world that I am privileged to see. This may seem dramatic, but it sure gives me a dose of reality and the motivation I need to jump out of bed and be thankful and happy for my job.

◄ ASK YOURSELF ►

- What aspects of my job do I enjoy most?

- If I'm feeling unmotivated or overwhelmed, how can I reframe the way I think about work?

- What are three things I am grateful for at work?

There is *luxury*
in simplicity.

UNKNOWN

USE AFFIRMATIONS AND MOTIVATIONAL QUOTES

Affirmations are subliminal statements you can use to enhance your work motivation, increase your productivity, or even discover joy in your work life. Many people fail to celebrate their talents, efforts, and overall life. By making affirmations part of your daily routine, you will notice that you focus more on the joyful aspects of your day versus all of the things you felt were failures. Positive affirmations work side by side with your subconscious to keep your mind motivated and focused on your goals.

I like to recite affirmations to myself before I begin my workday. This simple act has totally changed my day! This is why I love posting short ones on my social media each morning: That way, my followers have a dose of inspiration to start their day too. There are so many social media accounts you can follow that are filled with inspirational morning quotes to keep your feed flooded with positivity! I recommend staying away from the news or even television before you start your workday, as they both have the potential to draw you into something that will dampen your spirit and decrease your motivation.

Nikki's Favorite Affirmations

"I'M WORTH IT!"

*This affirmation lets you know that you deserve
all of the great things that life has to offer.*

"I'M TALENTED AND PROUD OF MY ACCOMPLISHMENTS."

*Remind yourself that you're good at what you do
and that you earned your achievements!*

"I'M CAPABLE OF DOING WHATEVER I SET MY MIND TO,
AND I CAN OVERCOME ANY CHALLENGE THROWN MY WAY."

*Sometimes we need motivators to remember that
we have what it takes to handle hurdles at work.*

"I GO WITH THE FLOW SO MY LIFE CAN BE EASY AND CALM."

*We all dislike the stressful feeling of running late to work.
If you are feeling out of control and completely stressed out,
recite a message like this one to center yourself in the morning.*

"I SEE AND FEEL THE BEAUTY IN THIS WORLD,
AND I AM JOYFUL."

*Try to take some time each day to enjoy nature and the beautiful views
around you. Maybe it's a few minutes in the morning or as you're driving to
work. You can enjoy wonderful things in this world—the sky, trees, birds—
by simply granting yourself the time to celebrate them!*

Remember, as you move forward on this journey of creating a beautifully organized workspace and work life, don't get discouraged. Just as your job required
experience and training, so does organization and shifting your mindset. These
are skills that must be honed over time. And believe it or not, the first step to
honing them starts at home.

CHAPTER TWO

WORK-LIFE ESSENTIALS

Throughout the years running my professional organizing business, I have always aimed to create a workspace where my team can feel comfortable and look forward to coming to the office each day. My goal is to create an environment that sets my employees up for success and allows them to do their best work.

That said, how well we perform at work often depends on how well we manage our lives outside the office. That's why I have often found that moms make the best employees. Why? Because multitasking is their specialty. Not only do moms have great time-management skills, but organizing seems to be their second language. That is a must in my field.

When I first started my business, the majority of my team members were young adults in their 20s who were living their best lives. They had no kids and no spouses, and some of them even still lived at home with their parents. While they were better at technology than I'll ever be, many of them were still learning how to stay organized and juggle the demands of adult life.

Meanwhile, I had another employee with children—three kids, plus 6 months pregnant with her fourth—whose husband had been deployed to Iraq and extended family all lived on the other side of the United States. She had a lot on her plate! And yet she was never late for work.

Each day when I walked into the office, I could rely on two things: the smell of freshly percolated coffee and this employee's upbeat attitude. She would have me laughing all the way to my office with her cheerful demeanor and bright personality.

One day at lunch, our team started discussing their daily routines. I was eager to have this team member share her secret to work-life success with the younger employees—and me. I told her how impressed I was that she was always the light of the office, given that she had so much to juggle outside of work.

So, what was her secret? She said it all boiled down to creating a routine that enabled her to start and end her day beautifully and stress free. This goes to show that no matter your situation, your effort to create a work-life routine has a huge impact on not only your day, but also the day of anyone who comes in contact with you.

Does your life feel unbalanced? Are you tired most of the time? Does your never-ending to-do list at work and at home get the best of you? If your answer is yes to any of these questions, then try to go easy on yourself. Remember that taking care of yourself, your family, and your home is a full-time job in and of itself. Having a career that takes up several hours of your day on top of your other demands can often cause a huge imbalance in your life and result in a lot of stress. That's why you need to take some steps to bring balance into your home and work life.

I often hear people say that there is no such thing as work-life balance, and I have to admit that I was once one of those people. But I have since come to realize that work-life balance is achievable if we make the right choices and implement systems that help us foster a happy medium. In this chapter, I share valuable tips to help organize your routine for a well-balanced and productive start to your day.

SET YOURSELF UP FOR SUCCESS

Depending on the type of job you have, your work schedule may start early in the morning, midday, or at night. You may have to commute to work, or perhaps you work right at home. But no matter when or where you start your workday, having a well-planned routine is key to setting yourself up for success. I recommend doing the following activities to establish your routine.

Create a routine list. Carve out a little time one day to sit down and make a master task list of all the things you need to accomplish before you head to work each day. Include everything: getting dressed, exercising, eating breakfast, showering, etc. Don't leave out any detail that requires time. I also recommend encouraging family members to make their own lists, especially if you start your days at the same time.

Assign times. Once you have your routine list completed, assign times to each item. Be generous with the times. It is always better to have more time than less! Assigning times to your routine is essential for accountability. It's easy to make lists, but to make them successful, you need to incorporate time limits. I've found that doing this prevents me from lagging behind and spending too much time on any one thing. If I didn't set time limits for myself, for instance, I might spend too long getting ready, and then I might not be able to leave when I should.

Schedule your tasks. For tasks that take the most time, consider adding them as recurring events on your calendar for each workday. Set an alarm notification for each time. This will give you your own personal assistant to keep you on schedule before you reach the office. Thanks to technology, you can even have a bit of fun with it. There are great home devices, such as the Amazon Echo and Google Nest, you can use to set upbeat reminders to help move your day along. If you have children, you can use these reminders to help keep them on schedule as well.

Sample Routine

MAKE THE BED

Making your bed can give you an immediate sense of accomplishment at the start of your day. It is a well-invested few minutes of your time.

2 MINUTES

DRINK WATER

Hydrating will help get your blood flowing and your face glowing. Save time by keeping a bottle of water at your bedside.

1 MINUTE

PRAY / MEDITATE / JOURNAL

One way to start your day on a positive note is to pray, meditate, or journal. This will give you a sense of peace and calm and help set the tone for your entire day and mood. It can also jump-start your creativity.

5 MINUTES

EXERCISE

If you want more energy and a way to relieve stress, then exercising—even for just a few minutes—is essential.

20 MINUTES

SHOWER

Showering before work not only ensures great hygiene, but is also an opportunity to invigorate your mind and body for your workday. Use proven energizing products, such as eucalyptus, orange, and lemon. Hanging fresh eucalyptus in your shower is also a great way to perk up!

5–10 MINUTES

GROOM YOURSELF

Creating a grooming caddy is a great way to keep this process simplified. Set up a small makeup caddy that includes only your everyday work makeup. This will eliminate having to rifle through drawers or bags to find what you need.

20 MINUTES

EAT BREAKFAST

Breakfast is such an important meal! Try not to skip it. Not only does it provide your body with energy to start your day, but eating breakfast can also help you concentrate.

15 MINUTES

GET DRESSED

If you prepare your outfit the night before, then getting dressed shouldn't take more than 10 minutes each day.

10 MINUTES

WAKE UP

I've never liked the idea of a traditional alarm clock. Who wants to be woken up while sleeping soundly by a loud, startling ring? That is a surefire way to raise your blood pressure and stress level, if you ask me. Here are some alternatives.

- Invest in a gentle-wake alarm clock. These clocks use light, vibration, or scent to wake you up.

- Take the time to train yourself to wake up naturally. I must note that this can be risky if you have a busy or regimented schedule. But if you are interested in giving it a try, there are several resources online that will walk you through the process.

- Invest in a smart mattress with features that wake you up gently by regulating the mattress temperature.

- Recruit a family member to help. What better way to wake up than with a beautiful kiss from your significant other? Your fur babies are also a viable option.

- Avoid checking social media and e-mail when you first wake up. The quickest way to get off track is to look at your phone. Instead, allow yourself a few extra minutes when you get to your office to check your phone and see what e-mails you need to address. Don't allow yourself to make excuses—"I just need to check the weather." That's a trap! If you need that kind of information, use a home device, such as an Amazon Echo, to give you the weather update for the day.

> **TIP**
>
> If you struggle to get up or feel exhausted throughout the day, you might not be getting enough sleep. If you struggle to sleep at night because you're thinking about your to-do list, keep a notebook and pen by your bed, and dump any thoughts into the notebook. That way, you'll clear them from your mind.

MAKE YOUR BED

Making your bed is one of the most important ways to start your day. Why? Because it's actually been proven to help people feel productive and happier, and then carry that attitude into their days. Sit up in bed and straighten your sheet and comforter. (Yes, while you are still in it!) Once you get out of bed, simply fix anything that's still out of place, and tuck your sheets under your mattress. You'll feel really accomplished in just 2 minutes!

SHOWER AND GROOM YOURSELF

Showering and grooming each day can be very time consuming, but I have learned some quick tricks to speed up the process.

- Use a microfiber towel to dry your hair. Because it absorbs water fast, it will speed up your drying time. Invest in a high-powered hair dryer, such as a Dyson, to greatly reduce your drying time. Yes, it's pricey, but their claim to fame is that you can dry your hair six times faster than with a normal dryer, and it works.

- Keep it simple. A minimal workday look can take you far! A good rule of thumb is to give 30 percent effort to your hair and makeup/grooming and 70 percent effort to your clothing. How you dress can have a bigger impact on your workday than adding extra layers of mascara.

- Minimize your options. Create a small kit that holds only the tools you need for your workday look. Don't include any of the extra items you use for going out or special occasions. Limit yourself to one of each item: one lipstick, one foundation, one eye shadow, etc. (or for the gentlemen, one beard oil, hair gel, etc.). The fewer options you have, the fewer decisions you have to make and the less time you have to spend.

- Consider getting multiple uses out of one item. For instance, there are some liquid blushes that double as lipstick and eye shadow. Or you can combine your face moisturizer with your foundation when you apply it, which can save you application time and extend the life of your foundation.

GET DRESSED

Reducing the number of pieces in your work wardrobe can make the process of getting dressed very simple, because fewer articles of clothing means less time deciding what to wear. You could think of your work outfits as a uniform, selecting pieces that all match or come from a similar color palette. You can also think about wearing dresses more often, which eliminates having to match a blouse to pants or a skirt. Here are some other tips.

- Select your clothing the night before. This can lessen a lot of frustration and time and prevent you from stressing out trying to decide what to wear each day. If you live in an area where the weather is unpredictable, give yourself two options just in case.

- When choosing your clothes, always make your shoes part of the process so you won't end up spending 15 minutes trying to find the perfect pair to go with your outfit.

- To save time on matching socks, stick with the same style, brand, and neutral color. That way, you don't have to worry about looking for a match that's gone missing.

- Install a hook in your closet where you can hang your work outfit each night and have it waiting for you the next morning. I like to think of it as my personal butler handing me my outfit for the day.

- Use sorting trays to organize your jewelry by color, and then coordinate pieces with your work attire. Consider choosing your jewelry the night before, after you have chosen the next day's outfit.

ORGANIZE YOUR WORKBAG

I'm always asked what I carry in my workbag, and my answer is simple: all of the things I need to make my workday easier and more convenient. My workbag is basically a mini version of my office. I have my personal assistant, IT department, break room, and conference room all in one place!

Although everyone's workbag may look different, it's important to purchase a durable bag that will last you a long time. After all, you will be using it heavily each day! Make sure it can hold the weight of all your items and manage being constantly carried around. I like to find bags with thick handles and shoulder straps, plenty of interior room, and side pockets to hold smaller items.

Organize your bag in a way that allows you to easily access any item. One way to ensure ease of use is to create "departments" within your bag. I do this

by using several mini bags or cases that can hold everything I need and also ensure direct and quick access to those items. I suggest the following departments, but remember, your workbag should only contain items that will help you function throughout your workday.

Tech area: I have a pocket or pouch for all of my tech items, such as headphones, a phone charger, and a camera. This helps me keep them secure and easy to find.

Supplies pouch: I have one case in my purse that holds any office supplies I might need on the go, such as pens, markers, and highlighters. Keeping them secure in a small pouch also prevents tops from coming loose and writing instruments from marking up the inside of my bag.

Planner and supplies: In addition to keeping my planners in my workbag, I also have another small pouch that contains all of the stickers, sticky notes, and notepads I use for planning.

Hygiene and makeup bag: I keep a small bag in my workbag with hand sanitizer, lipstick, lotion, female hygiene items, and anything else I might need to feel good throughout the day

Eyeglasses or sunglasses case: I always want to keep my glasses in a case to keep them safe and easy to find in my bag. I like to keep a wipe inside the case as well so I can clean them whenever I need to.

Side pockets: I select a workbag that has several side pockets to hold my smartphone, wallet, business card holder, and keys. That way, these frequently used items are easy to grab on the go.

Small purse: I like to have room for a small purse in case I need to make any quick trips during the day and don't want to lug my heavy workbag around.

Laptop bag: If you carry a laptop with you, make sure it has its own case or sleeve and can easily fit either in your bag or under your arm.

PLAN YOUR BREAKFAST AND LUNCH

Rather than asking yourself what you want for breakfast or lunch every single day, use these tips to save yourself some time.

- Plan your breakfast the night before or get into a routine of eating the same two or three items each week so you don't have to think about it. Select recipes or grab-and-go items that you can easily make or throw into your bag in a pinch. This will give you more time to enjoy your family's company before work or start planning your schedule for the day. I've included some tasty, easy-to-make recipes that you can prepare in advance.

- Use a programmable coffee maker. Talk about a motivator! Who doesn't love waking up to freshly brewed coffee? Keep your coffee cup and travel mug next to your coffee maker to save another step.

- Pack your lunch the night before. This will give you one less thing to think about before your workday. Then when you're at work, use lunch as a time to rest and recharge—not multitask! We all need a break and it's important to give yourself a proper one. You deserve it!

Breakfast Parfait

INGREDIENTS

- 1 cup yogurt
- ½ cup fresh berries
- ½ cup granola

PREPARATION

1. Spoon a layer of yogurt in the bottom of a cup or mason jar.

2. Place a layer of berries on top.

3. Sprinkle granola on top of the berries.

4. Repeat until the cup or jar is full.

5. Cover the cup or jar with a piece of plastic wrap or lid and place in the fridge overnight.

Overnight Oats

INGREDIENTS

- ½ cup old-fashioned rolled oats
- ½ cup milk
- ½ teaspoon sugar, honey, or other sweetener
- ¼ teaspoon vanilla extract
- Dash of cinnamon (optional)
- Berries, almond butter, and almonds, for topping (optional)

PREPARATION

1. Add all the ingredients but the toppings to a small mason jar. Secure the lid on top and shake well.

2. Place the jar in the fridge and let it rest for at least 6 hours.

3. When ready to eat, top the oats with your favorite toppings, such as berries, almond butter, or almonds.

4. The mixture can stay fresh in the refrigerator for up to 4 days.

LEAVE FOR WORK

Before I head out the door for the day, I like to do a final check to make sure I have everything I need and I'm not forgetting anything. These tips have really helped me make sure I'm good to go.

- Hang a whiteboard on your front or back door and use it to leave messages for family members the night before so you don't have to remember to tell them the next day.

- Create a "forget-me-not" basket or bin and keep it next to your front or back door. Put any items you need to take to work in the basket. This will minimize the number of items you need to track down before you leave.

- If you packed a lunch, create a card that says, "Get your lunch!" and keep it in your basket to remind you to grab your food before you head out the door.

- If you tend to lose your keys, always keep them in your forget-me-not basket so you know exactly where they are. You might also consider investing in a smart tracker, such as Tile, that allows you to use your phone to locate your keys, should they ever go missing.

- Place your workbag and/or handbag next to your forget-me-not basket. That way, it will be easy to grab your bag as you head out the door.

TIP

Before you start your workweek, be sure to fill up your gas tank. That way, you'll have one less thing on your to-do list during a busy week.

PLAN YOUR COMMUTE

Finally, if you have a commute to work, I encourage you to consider how you spend that time in your vehicle. What mood are you creating, and how is it setting the tone for the rest of your day?

Choose your audio wisely: I like to listen to relaxing, inspirational music—soft jazz or an artist like Norah Jones. Or I might listen to an inspirational audiobook or podcast that helps motivate me, teach me something new, and put me in the right mindset for work. I know it's tempting to listen to the news or talk radio, but I would advise you to reconsider, because that kind of noise is most likely going to increase your heart rate and stress you out.

Use aromatherapy: Do you keep an air freshener in your car? I like to use ones with aromatherapy scents, such as lavender. You can also find car aromatherapy diffusers at stores such as Bed Bath & Beyond.

Get inspired: As I mentioned in Chapter 1, reading affirmations before work provides an opportunity for a moment of calm before you tackle your day. I like to keep a book of inspirational quotes in my glove box so I have something to look at before I walk into the office. If you don't travel by car, you might want to keep a small book like this on your desk in your home office, or follow a few motivational social media accounts that you can look at before starting your day.

CHAPTER THREE

ORGANIZING YOUR PHYSICAL WORKSPACE

I once had a client whose workspace looked like it could have been a warehouse for Staples. She had multiples of every office supply you could possibly imagine and admitted that she was the "queen of catching a great bulk sale."

Her desk was showered with stacks of papers. She had one bin for her incoming mail, another for her outgoing mail, and several other bins for all of her assignments and projects. The average person walking into her space would have immediately felt overwhelmed. Unfortunately, so did she. She confessed that her current approach to organization was stressing her out and creating more confusion than clarity. Thankfully, I knew just how to help. It was time to get to work!

I grabbed a small bin and asked her to "shop" her office for all of the items she felt she needed to get through a typical workday. As she walked through the space, she gathered her pens, her Post-its, and several other office supplies. I then asked her to grab one letter tray (she had at least 20) and told her we were all set with what she needed. She looked at me like I was from a different planet.

Instead of having 20 trays, I told her that she should instead put all of her items in one tray and call it her "action file." She would then only need to work from one location. She thought this was a temporary step. Little did she know that this would be her new working system, because it took her mind from having to focus on 20 piles of papers and responsibilities to just one.

As the week went on, her office clutter decreased significantly and her finances increased as we sorted through and sold off excess supplies and equipment. When we were done, she realized that she was still able to function in her office. Not only that, she was actually able to get more work done with fewer items. Once we had cleared her office clutter, we were able to have fun focusing on the other elements of her office: selecting ideal lighting and a nice lamp for her desk, procuring her dream office chair, and even picking out the perfect plant for her desk.

To this day, she continues to work in a beautifully organized office—one that has just one drawer of office supplies and one active to-do file. The only thing that's changed is the joy she now has in her voice. By helping her understand that it takes very little to accomplish great things and it's important to set limits to prevent clutter and create focus, she now has a soothing, functioning work environment.

A cluttered office can be summed up in two words: *stress and frustration.* That is why creating a beautifully organized workspace is essential not only to your productivity but also to your health. Walking into a work environment filled with clutter and disorganization breeds more stress day after day, and that stress will inevitably transfer over to your home life and impact your well-being and the well-being of your family.

In this chapter, I will share simple tips to bring long-lasting function and beauty to your physical workspace. These techniques have worked for hundreds of my clients, and I know they can work for you, too. Throughout the book, you'll see that I employ the same 5-step system that I used for your home in *Beautifully Organized*: Assess, declutter, clean, organize, beautify. Now I want you to apply it to your workspace.

STEP ONE: ASSESS

Before you even begin decluttering and reorganizing, I think it's important to look at your space as a whole and assess the three core office items that most impact your comfort: your desk, chair, and lighting. Regardless of whether you are working at home or in an office, tailoring these items to your needs should be among your top priorities.

DESK ► Today, there are a variety of desk options to fit every work need. When you look for your ideal desk, it's important to consider what you think will work best for your situation.

- *Ergonomics:* You may spend hours sitting at your desk and not realize the long-term health implications on your body. It is important to se-

lect a desk that's at the right height for you—one that minimizes pain and keeps your energy levels up. You may even want to consider an adjustable-height desk if you want a setup that allows you to alternate between sitting and standing throughout the day.

- **Storage:** The second important factor when selecting a desk is storage. I used to work at my dining room table, and while it was beautiful, it didn't offer any drawers for me to securely store my things. I know some offices provide employees with just a simple table without any desk drawers, but if you do have them, they are critical for stowing away your office supplies and helping prevent clutter from piling up on top of your desk.

- **Style:** A desk doesn't have to be anything fancy. Remember, think about function first! *Then* consider how you can style it to your liking. A few years ago, my husband and I found a nice, sturdy wooden desk with plenty of drawers at Goodwill for under three dollars! After a fresh coat of white paint, that old desk looked brand new and fit perfectly into my office aesthetic.

- **Positioning:** I am big on office feng shui, and I've learned that one of the most important things to keep in mind is that the position of your desk can affect your performance. Now, I know that not everyone has a choice of where their desk goes (maybe your space doesn't allow for flexibility), but if you do have the option, make sure your desk is facing forward, toward the energy of the room, not up against a wall, where you can't see your surroundings.

CHAIR ▶ Just as it can be beneficial to have a desk that encourages good ergonomics, the same is true for your office chair. Remember, you will probably spend hours sitting in this chair, so you want it to not only be comfortable but also provide good back support and allow you to adjust it to the perfect height for working at your desk. A good desk chair isn't always cheap, but this isn't something to skimp on. Here are some things to keep in mind.

- **Height:** Is the height adjustable? You want your thighs to be parallel to the floor and your arms within easy reach of your desk.

- **Support:** Does it have lumbar support? Try out a few chairs and select one that naturally aligns with the contour of your spine and gives it the support it needs.

- **Armrests:** Does it have adjustable armrests? Armrests take some of the pressure off your neck and shoulders as you're working throughout the day.

- **Movement:** Does it move easily? A chair with wheels and swiveling capacity is more functional than a dining chair that doesn't move at all.

LIGHTING ▸ Offices often have ugly fluorescent lighting that makes the space look like an interrogation room. This drives me crazy! Lighting is everything in a workspace, especially when it comes to creating a warm and relaxed vibe that keeps you calm and focused.

Studies have shown that one-third of workers would be happier if they had better lighting in their office. This puts lighting at the top of the list when it comes to a well-organized office! Lighting not only impacts your mood but also plays a huge role in how productive and creative you are at work.

LED lights are very popular these days, because they are more energy efficient and have a longer life span, which often saves businesses money. They are also healthier for employees since fluorescent lights can cause headaches for some people, which definitely affects productivity.

When choosing lighting for your office, it is important to think about not only your tasks but also your well-being. There are three lighting types that I feel are necessary to create an overall cohesive and motivating experience during your workday.

NATURAL LIGHTING

- gives you energy
- keeps you alert and improves overall mood
- great for private offices and workspaces

BLUE/COOL LIGHTING

- increases productivity
- saves energy
- great for spaces that require high productivity (such as brainstorming) and general-use spaces (restroom, copier room, etc.)

ORANGE/WARM LIGHTING

- creates a sense of comfort
- makes your workspace feel more welcoming
- great for intimate settings, such as the break room or reception area

If you can choose where you work, I recommend putting natural light at the top of your list. Since not everyone has control over the amount of natural light in their workspace, though, the next best thing you can do is consider the type of light bulb.

Here are some factors to consider.

- *Be sure to choose the right-sized bulb.* If you have a bigger office, you can use a bigger bulb; if you have a smaller office, choose a smaller bulb.

- *Consider a light bulb with speakers.* This will allow you to enjoy personalized work music along with your chosen lighting. Companies such as Sengled have great options.

- *Programmable lighting* is a great option that gives you control over your lighting throughout the day.

As I mentioned earlier, one way to balance out bad lighting is to always have a lamp on your desk. A lamp has always been a staple for me, whether I'm working in a cubicle or a private office. This type of intimate lighting buffers the harshness of those overhead lights and gives you a nice, warm work environment.

HOW TO CHOOSE THE PERFECT DESKTOP LAMP

- Be sure to choose the correct height. The lamp should be taller than your head when you're sitting at your desk and not be level with your eyes.

- You should also ensure the light does not create a shadow on your desktop. Move it as needed to make sure the light isn't overshadowing the part of the desk where you work.

- Make sure you can easily reach the switch to turn the lamp on or off. Consider a lamp with a pull chain.

STEP TWO: *DECLUTTER*

Once you have assessed the essentials in your office, it's time to dive into decluttering. Most of my clients are very frustrated with their workspace and don't know where to begin, so it's important for me to give them a boost of inspiration and motivation in the beginning—something that shows them they can have beautiful order at work.

The physical desktop is a simple place to start. Most people will look at their desk, shake their heads, and say, "Not mine!" Yes, yours. The first thing I do is work with my client to clear their desktop by placing all items on the floor—or in a different area, in categories, so as not to create a total disaster.

When they see that empty desktop, they see hope. Giving my clients a look at what they can have right at the beginning is hugely beneficial and gets them excited about having an organized workspace. It's kind of like having dessert before dinner!

There are a few reasons your desk is the perfect place to start. Just like the entryway to your home, your desk is the first thing that welcomes you as you start work. It is your first impression of your day. When you arrive at your desk and see disorganization and clutter, it slowly but surely starts to transfer productivity into stress. Organizing your desktop is a great place to start, because it may seem overwhelming, but it is actually a quick project that will produce a huge dose of motivation.

1. Stand in front of your desk with a trash bin and throw away anything that you see as trash. Don't go digging for trash! Only toss out trash that is apparent.

2. Take all the items that fall into the office supply category and place them in one pile on the floor or in a vacant area of your office.

3. Take all the paperwork on your desk and put it in another pile on the floor. (Don't worry about categorizing at this point.)

4. Take any décor items and place them in one pile on the floor.

5. Take any tech items and place them in one pile on the floor.

Once you have all of the items in piles, away from your desk, take the opportunity to enjoy the moment of visual minimalism. (Just don't look at the floor!)

STEP THREE: *CLEAN*

Once your desk is cleared off, wipe it down with cleaner and sanitizing wipes. I recommend having wipes in your office at all times to clean up any spills, stains, or stickiness, which inevitably happen if you are drinking coffee or eating lunch there. I have an end-of-day cleaning routine I do each evening before I leave my office, which you'll learn more about at the end of this chapter.

STEP FOUR: *ORGANIZE*

Now that everything has been removed, it's time to ask yourself what really deserves to earn its place back on your desk.

TOP OF DESK ▶

- **The essentials:** What do you need most to do your work throughout the day? I like to keep my planner, notebook, smartphone, and computer on my desk and easily accessible. I also use my (clean!) notebook as a mouse pad, giving it dual functionality.

- **Desk tray or supply holder:** Use a desk tray to store often-used office supplies—stapler, penholder, tape dispenser—neatly on one surface of your desk. That way, they don't end up scattered all over the place

- **Office supplies:** I have always invested in my own office supplies so I have the look I want and supplies that function the way I want them to. I've never liked to settle for whatever the office provides. Make sure the supplies that you select for the top of your desk are attractive and coordinated, and that they complement your desired room decor.

- **Desk accessories:** I've used a clear bowl and even a champagne glass to hold pens, pencils, and clips. Something atypical like this can bring a lot of style to your desk in addition to being functional. Acrylic accessories are beautiful and unbreakable, and they help keep the space from feeling overwhelming.

- **_Desk calendar:_** Writing your schedule on a desk calendar may be helpful, but it can also clutter the appearance of your workspace. To keep your desk looking neat and tidy, my advice is to always keep the top page blank.

- ***Stickies notebook:*** In my opinion, sticky notes are one of the fastest ways to clutter and overwhelm your desk. If you use them, purchase a small blank journal or notebook where you can safely store them in one place for easy access. Even though the journal/notebook serves as a beautiful disguise for your notes, be sure to detox and toss the ones you no longer need at the end of each day.

- ***Work pile covers:*** Sometimes, keeping paper on your desk is inevitable. But how you display it can make all the difference! I like to buy simple decorative file folders, which I use as covers for my piles of work. These go on top of my piles so I see the pretty covers on top rather than the work itself. (This creates a more streamlined look too.) Each one is labeled—Urgent, To-do, File—so I know the task at hand and can keep things organized. When I walk into my office in the morning, I don't want to see everything that needs to be done staring me down! This system prevents messy piles from slapping me in the face, plus it's good for confidentiality. And when I walk into the office, I know that the urgent pile is what I need to address first. Everything has its place.

Once you have addressed the essentials on top of your desk, it's time to turn to what's in your storage spaces.

DESK DRAWERS OR CABINET STORAGE ▸ If you have a desk with drawers, it is important to establish a category for each drawer. This helps keep your desk organized, because everything has a home within it, and you know exactly where everything belongs. If your desk doesn't have drawers, consider purchasing a small cabinet with storage to stow away everything you need.

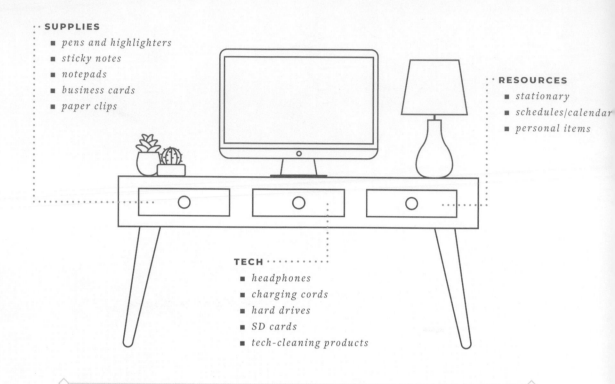

SUPPLIES
- *pens and highlighters*
- *sticky notes*
- *notepads*
- *business cards*
- *paper clips*

RESOURCES
- *stationary*
- *schedules/calendar*
- *personal items*

TECH
- *headphones*
- *charging cords*
- *hard drives*
- *SD cards*
- *tech-cleaning products*

I created the diagram above to show you three core areas to organize. To maximize the space in your drawers, I also recommend using drawer organizers, if possible.

- **SUPPLIES:** In this drawer, I keep my general supplies, pads, business cards, rulers, washi tape, and paper clips—everything I use on a daily basis. It stays neat so I know exactly where everything is.

- **TECH:** This drawer houses all my tech equipment in one place. No more losing important cords or chargers!

- **RESOURCES:** Finally, in my third drawer are any company resources or important business items. I also make space here for personal items that can help refresh me throughout the day, such as makeup or lotion.

FILE CABINETS ▸ A file cabinet or file drawer is essential for storing your most essential documents. There are so many options! Choose what works best for you. That could be a traditional file cabinet, a file box, a file accordion, a magazine rack, or a file cart.

There is no one way that works best to organize files across the board. Each person and company is different and has different needs. What is important is

that you have some type of structure when organizing files. It may vary, but the structure must be present to have an organized filing system.

Here is how I keep my own files organized, which I encourage you to do as well.

1. Start by writing a list of the categories needed in the file cabinet. This will serve as your road map. Be sure to keep the names of the files simple and easy to understand.

2. Create a color-coded system for each category. For example:
    a. Red file: Clients
    b. Blue file: Suppliers and vendors
    c. Green file: Company documents

3. File items in their respective categories in the file cabinet.

Some other key things to remember when you set up your file cabinet:

- Don't mix business files with personal ones.

- Keep spare files in the cabinet in case a new file needs to be set up in the future.

- Keep a "quick file" in the front of your file cabinet for items you reference frequently.

One alternative to traditional filing is to create a binder system, another favorite of mine. Buy a set of binders in different colors and properly label them the same way you would file folders. I keep these in a deep desk drawer, where I can easily pull them out. Binders also make it easier to pass important files along to someone else on your team whenever needed. It's also a good idea to get a set of plastic sleeves to hold your documents within each binder. To make it easy to find a specific binder, I like to buy metal nameplates at the supply store and use them to professionally label each binder on the outside.

FILE MAINTENANCE ▸ Setting up your work files is a much easier task than maintaining your file drawer. I find that many people have a hard time keeping an organized filing system because of the maintenance it requires, not because of how the system is set up. For this reason, I have found that many people are more successful when they create a maintenance system that does not require them to continually file things.

I like the concept of keeping one active "file" inbox on your desk. As papers come in

that need to be filed, simply place them in this box. Set aside 15 minutes at the end of each workweek to close out your office. This simple planning session will help you remedy that large file of papers that always seems to be sitting on your desk.

Each Friday before leaving work, file all of the papers in their proper places, and then clean your desk and office area before you leave for the day. Filing your paperwork is like doing the dishes. You do not want to walk into a mess on Monday morning! Knowing that you will be filing every Friday afternoon relieves you from "inbox guilt." You have taken control and scheduled this task! The key is to be consistent, closing out your active file each week.

STEP FIVE: *BEAUTIFY*

Once your workspace is organized, the next step is to personalize it and make it special. Here are some of my favorite tips.

SELF-CARE STATION ▸
Create a self-care station in your desk drawer organizer, where you'll keep items such as your favorite hand cream, lip balm, and nail clippers. Having these items easily accessible will provide a pick-me-up whenever you need it and ensure you are presentable for any impromptu meeting or video call. You can also create a little beverage station and include things such as your favorite tea bags and sugar packets.

FAMILY PHOTOS ▸ We all love to display pictures of family, but be careful not to overwhelm your desk with too many photos. To save space, get a frame that has places to showcase several photos.

MIRROR ▸ If your desk is up against a wall, I encourage you to place a mirror or mirrored picture frame against your desk so you can see if someone is coming up on you. This will also help the space feel bigger.

AROMATHERAPY / CALMING SCENTS ▸ Use a mini perfume bottle to store your favorite linen spray, and use it to boost your energy throughout the day. Use scents that awaken, such as citrus; save the lavender for your bedside table. You might also want to consider keeping an essential oil diffuser on your desktop. (Just make sure whatever scent you select doesn't bother others in your office.) I also encourage you to place scent sacks inside your desk drawers and file cabinets. That way, you will smell the relaxing scent every time you open a drawer—a small breath of fresh air during a stressful workday.

Every day, before I leave the office, I also put a couple of drops of essential oil on my desk and wipe it down. This creates a nice, subtle scent that greets me when I return in the morning.

CANDLES ▸ If your office allows the use of candles, they can be a great way to reduce stress while working. If you're using other scents in your office, consider an unscented candle. Setting the tone for your day is huge. I believe it's all in the details! It's important that we do these small things to have a stress-free and relaxed work environment each day.

PLANTS ▸ I like to have at least one plant in my office, even though I'm not always great at keeping them alive! Plants are purifying and bring a great vibe to any space. Lately, I've been trying to decorate with succulents.

MUSIC ▸ If you like to work with music on, I recommend playing some ambient sounds in the background, either through a speaker or earbuds. You might be tempted to listen to your favorite albums at work, but opt for soft music or sounds that keep you relaxed, especially if you work around others. You might also consider a sound machine that plays natural noises, such as a gentle rainfall or ocean tide.

DÉCOR ▸ Choose the art for your office carefully. What can you display that will be calming or uplifting? I like to decorate with tranquil blues and teals, because they represent peace to me and help me concentrate. Research feng shui colors and see if there is a particular one that might work well for you. Affirmation wall art can also be motivating. (Remember those affirmations we talked about in the last chapter?) Surround yourself with words from your favorite thought leaders who inspire you.

PRIOR TO LEAVING WORK

Before you leave work, take 5 minutes to organize your workspace for the next day. Preparing the night before can ensure the following workday gets started on the right foot. Use these tips to simplify the process.

CLEAN UP YOUR TECH ▸ Is the desktop on your computer cluttered to the point that you can no longer see your wallpaper? Does it take you longer than 8 seconds to find a file on your computer? These issues cause stress and

are huge time wasters. Take a minute to sort out your files at the end of each day, which will enable you to keep your computer organized at all times. In the next chapter, I will talk in more detail about how to organize your digital work life, but for now, focus on taking a few minutes before you end work each day to clear out what you don't need and make what you do need easier to find.

CLEAN YOUR KEYBOARD ► Turn your keyboard upside down and shake it to remove any debris. Keep a toothbrush in your desk drawer specifically for getting out dust from your keyboard and tech items. Alcohol wipes are also great for cleaning makeup and other markings off your keyboard. A budget-friendly alternative to wipes is to fill a mini perfume spray bottle with alcohol and spray it onto cotton rounds whenever you need to wipe something down.

DISINFECT YOUR WORK AREA ► Take a minute to disinfect your personal workspace before you leave. Using a Lysol or Clorox wipe makes this task quick and easy. Or, if you prefer a more natural solution, a combination of water and vinegar will do the trick.

CLEAN YOUR COFFEE CUP ► Cleaning your coffee cup before you leave each day makes it easier to start your next morning at work. Sprinkle a little baking soda in your coffee cup and add a little water to make a paste, then rub the cup with it. This mixture will combat those coffee stains and keep your cup sparkling.

EMPTY YOUR TRASH ► Walking into work and being hit with the smell of yesterday's lunch is not the best way to boost your mood. If your office doesn't have a cleaning staff or you're working from home, this is one step you definitely don't want to skip! Make the process go faster by keeping a handful of trash bags in the bottom of your trash bin. That way, you can easily replace the trash bag. Note: Be sure to shred all sensitive information prior to disposing of it.

GIVE YOURSELF LOVE ► We do so much in a day that we often forget to do a small thing that makes a huge difference! Before you leave work each day, write yourself a positive note and place it on your desk. If you are a coffee drinker, perhaps place a securely wrapped biscotti beside the note. Remember, a little self-care goes a long way. Also, simply writing the note is a great way to transition from your work mindset to your home mindset as you leave each day.

CHAPTER FOUR

ORGANIZING YOUR DIGITAL WORKSPACE

I have to admit that I'm not the most technologically savvy person. I often get into a routine of doing something the hard way simply because it is more familiar or comfortable. For years, I was pretty stubborn about doing things my way when it came to technology, even if it was less efficient and reduced my productivity. But then I witnessed a conversation between two baby boomers (my father and father-in-law) that quickly changed my ways.

They were seeking driving directions to a nearby city and pulled out a foreign object: a map. I couldn't believe they had one in the days of smartphones and GPS technology. My initial thought was, *Wow, they still make those?* Then I watched as the two men spent 45 minutes studying the route on the map, even though they could have retrieved the same information in a few short minutes using their smartphones. In the time it took them to find their destination on the paper map, they probably could have driven there and back!

When my husband and I suggested that my father and father-in-law use their phones, both of them shook their heads and agreed that they preferred the paper map. Why? Because it was in their comfort zone. That's when I had a wake-up moment: I realized I was doing the same thing in many areas of *my* life. I needed to make a change.

I often also find this to be true when it comes to my clients and technology: They get so used to managing their digital files and documents in a particular way that even though their system makes it much harder for them to track down the files later, they stick with their method. Not only does this stubbornness waste time and money, but it also adds a tremendous amount of stress to your life.

In today's workplace, it is essential to access information quickly. That means keeping your digital files and devices clutter free. Clutter is not limited to what you see when you walk into your office! Digital clutter can cause you just as much stress and frustration.

Is your computer desktop completely covered with files? Are your important e-mails buried under a bunch of newsletters or unimportant memos? Can you never find the password you need? If so, this chapter will teach you how to declutter your tech life easily so you can maintain a functional digital workspace with minimal frustration.

COMPUTER DESKTOP

Creating a plan to keep your computer organized can bring order and function to your digital work life.

STEP ONE: *ASSESS*

Ask yourself what you use most frequently on your computer. What do you need quick and easy access to at all times? What files should be on your desktop?

STEPS TWO & THREE: *DECLUTTER AND CLEAN*

The first step is to block off some time to delete any folders or files you no longer need. If you have large files that you use infrequently, or have files which you're not sure whether you'll need again one day but would have trouble easily replacing, drop them all in a single folder and then back up that folder on an external hard drive or send them to the cloud so you can still access them, should you ever need to do so. (See more on this in the tip later in this section.)

STEP FOUR: *ORGANIZE*

Now that you have the files you need on your computer, it's time to label them properly. Create a naming system that allows you to immediately know what's in each folder—in other words, a system that won't create any confusion. You can also color-code your icons for easy identification.

Here are some tips for categorizing your files.

- Think about the process we used for organizing your physical desktop. Ask yourself, *What is most essential for me to see on my computer desktop each day?* Anything that's not essential should be stored away in folders.

- When it comes to naming folders, use clear language that will help you easily remember what's in them. Use full words instead of abbreviations you may not remember.

- When it comes to naming the files within folders, you also want to be very clear. Think about file naming as a version of communicating with your future self: You are leaving clues to help yourself find things. The less clear you are, the harder it will be to identify what those files are in the future. Adding dates or version numbers (v1, v2, v3) to your file names is also very helpful.

Screenshots are often one reason computer desktops become a cluttered mess! Remedy this by setting up your screenshots to be automatically routed to a screenshot folder on your desktop. There are several resources online that will walk you through this setup, depending on your computer system. Google "how to send screenshots to a specific folder."

CREATE A "TO BE ORGANIZED" FOLDER ▸ Just as you clean your desk at the end of your workday, you should also clean your computer desktop. Doing so means you will walk into a workspace that is both physically and digitally organized each day. I recommend creating a "to be organized" file on your desktop where you can drop in all items that need to be organized later. Then consider setting aside one time each week to do so.

TIP

Back up your files. These days, there is really no excuse not to back up your computer files, because almost all of us have access to the cloud. On a Mac, iCloud is a tool that will regularly back up files on your phone and computer. Google offers Google Drive, and Microsoft has OneDrive. That way, if your computer ever crashes or you lose your phone, you don't have to worry about losing all of your hard work.

STEP FIVE: *BEAUTIFY*

Now that you have the most important files on your computer desktop, the next step is to organize them so you can quickly find them again. One way I keep mine organized is by using a wallpaper organizer like the one on the next page. You can make one yourself if you are comfortable using design programs, such as Canva or Photoshop, or you can download a template online. Just do a Google search for "desktop wallpaper organizer."

Another option is to buy an external hard drive online or at your local electronics or office supply store. Make a habit of plugging it in at the end of each week and backing up your files so you have saved copies of your latest work.

Desktop Wallpaper Organizer

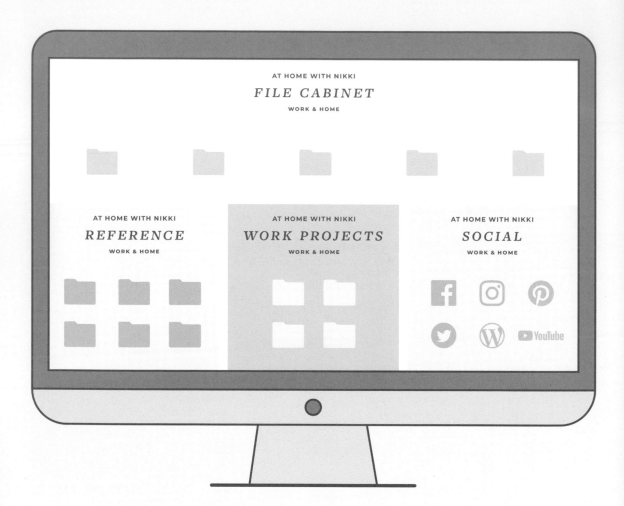

This type of wallpaper, which is simply a background image on your desktop, is one of the simplest ways to keep your items sorted. Make sure you keep your desktop wallpaper minimal and neutral, as busy desktop wallpaper can make it difficult to find your files, costing you time and energy.

E-MAIL

Sometimes reading and sorting e-mails can feel like a full-time job on its own. That's why it is important to implement systems to help you manage this huge daily task.

PRIORITIZING E-MAILS WITH THE 80/20 RULE ▶ I'm sure your inbox often becomes a black hole that sucks you in when you open it, causing your productivity to decrease. To better balance your workload, use the 80/20 rule when it comes to reading and responding to e-mails.

E-mails that pertain to your immediate work goals should be in the 20 percent category and addressed immediately. This may include e-mails about new business opportunities, new clients, or other urgent matters at your company. All other e-mails fall into the 80 percent category and can be addressed later. Whether you respond to them later in the day or later in the week will depend on the expectations of your manager.

- **20 percent category:** The most important e-mails that will make a big difference in your work goals should go here.

- **80 percent category:** There are two levels within this category.

  o *Level 1:* Important, but not as important as the e-mails in the 20 percent category. These e-mails keep work moving but aren't urgent. Spend time addressing them *after* you've prioritized your more important correspondence and work that day.

  o *Level 2:* Unimportant e-mails, such as fun reads, spam, or promotional e-mails

WHEN TO CHECK YOUR E-MAIL ▶ The reality is that your inbox is going to be flooded with new messages day and night. If you have alerts or notifica-

TIP

I also recommend the 1-minute rule. If it takes you only 1 minute to respond to an e-mail, then simply go ahead and respond. If it requires more time, use the 80/20 rule.

tions set up on your computer or phone, that means a *ding!* every time one of those new e-mails drops into your inbox. Talk about a distraction!

I encourage you to switch off e-mail alerts and notifications and instead set specific times to check your e-mail throughout the day. If you're constantly refreshing your inbox or clicking on new e-mails as they pop up on your screen, you will constantly be derailed from your other work. Think of keeping your e-mail alert on as the equivalent of being a switchboard operator: It means you have no time for anything else.

By selecting a few key times each day to check e-mail—maybe first thing in the morning when you start working, again at lunch, and again in the afternoon—you can stay in control of how you respond and manage your own time more effectively, keeping your mind freed up to focus on the work that matters most.

Whenever you're focused on important work, keep that inbox closed! It'll do wonders for your productivity.

SETTING E-MAIL FILTERS ▸ Setting up e-mail filters can be a great way to presort your e-mails so your inbox stays manageable. E-mails you receive on a consistent basis can be automatically filtered into their own folders. Google how to do this for the e-mail platform you use (Gmail, Outlook, Apple Mail). Filtering will allow you to control when you open and read your e-mails. This frees up time to handle more important messages.

CREATING AN E-MAIL SCHEDULER ▸ Your e-mail account should have a function that allows you to schedule when you send your e-mails. That means you can write them now and then they will only be sent to the recipients at your preferred time. I often schedule when my e-mails go out so I can control when I receive responses. This helps manage the number of new e-mails coming to me throughout the day and when they arrive. Another service offered by servers like Gmail is allowing you to write automatic replies that you can send again and again. These are prewritten messages that you send multiple times and are already saved; with the click of a button, your e-mail auto-populates with that text. This tool saves you the time of writing the same thing over and over again.

A FEW FINAL TIPS ▶

- **Go to Ohio.** Not the state, but the acronym: Only hold it once. Make a habit of reading an e-mail only once, and don't revisit it or push it off after you have opened it. Read it, and then decide at that moment whether to respond to it or put it into your 80 percent category to address later.

- **Keep work and personal e-mails separate.** Combining work and personal messages can create confusion. Messages about client meetings shouldn't be mixed up with e-mails about your child's piano lessons. Separate e-mail addresses and inboxes are essential for staying in control. Sorting e-mails wastes time; it's easier to have them separated from the beginning.

- **Write concise, easy-to-read e-mails.** Also use clear subject lines so you and the recipient can easily see what the e-mail is about at a glance. This clarity will also help you more easily find old e-mails in your own inbox and refer back to information faster whenever you need it.

- **Consider not sending an e-mail.** If you're not sure whether you need to send that e-mail, then maybe don't. One of the most surefire ways to receive fewer e-mails is to send fewer yourself!

If social media updates are another thing stealing your attention, turn those notifications off. I try to check social media at work only if it's *for* work. Keep the personal updates for outside office hours.

PASSWORDS

Passwords are another headache for many people. We waste so many minutes each day trying to remember passwords we created. You might even find yourself resetting your password frequently! What a stressor. And then there is password security you need to keep in mind so you don't worry about someone else logging in as you.

HOW TO CREATE A SECURE PASSWORD ▸ My best tip for creating a password is to create one single phrase and then alter it with symbols and numbers. Never use regular words, names, or birth dates

EXAMPLE:

I Will Always Love You = *Iwi11Alw@ysLoveYou*

Now you may be thinking, *How am I going to remember that?* I recommend using a password manager, such as LastPass or 1Password, to save and manage your passwords. These programs save all of your passwords and create a new master password that you can use across websites. That way, you only have to remember one password in the future.

PASSWORD KEEPER

mybeautifulsite.com
WEBSITE

myname
USERNAME

Whi!ney@work!
PASSWORD

work
E-MAIL LINKED

1 / 31 / 2025
MEMBERSHIP EXPIRATION DATE

If you are more of a pen-and-paper person, you can create a paper password notebook and keep it in a secure place. If you do this, though, never put the actual passwords in the notebook. Instead, use cryptic messaging only you understand that will help you quickly remember the password.

TECH EQUIPMENT ▸ Now that we have tackled getting your items decluttered and organized, it is time to move on to organizing your digital tech, which can clutter your workspace in the blink of an eye. On your desk, you may have a desktop computer for your main responsibilities, a laptop for mobile use, and, of course, your smartphone. These essentials all come with their own cords, accessories, and cases.

Cords are one of my least favorite things to see in an office, because they create an unsightly mess and clutter on the floor or behind your desk. Thankfully, I've created a system for labeling and hiding my cords and other tech equipment.

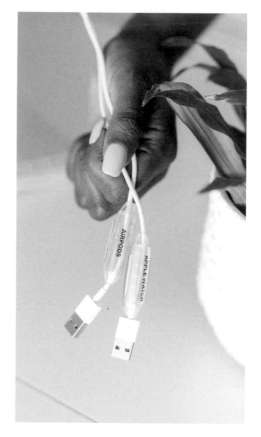

- *Labeling cords:* Tag your cords with label tape or cord label clips. I recommend Cord ID Pro, which I found on Amazon. These tags allow me to label my cords so I know which device each belongs to. I can then easily remove the label if I need to move or get rid of the cord.

- *Hiding cords:* I like to group cords at the base of the plug or surge protector and then use a zip tie to attach them to something, be it a desk leg or another piece of furniture. I just hate having the cords hanging on the floor, not to mention the tripping hazard they create! I also like to look for a bar or hidden back side of my desk that I can tape them to, or I'll use 3M Command strips so the cords are hidden from the eye and don't disrupt the look of my workspace. You can also use desk accessories, such as a pencil holder, lamp, or plant to conceal cords from your view.

- *Using a tech drawer or binder:* As I mentioned earlier, I like to keep all the cords and chargers that I don't use every day neatly organized in a tech drawer. Think of this as one central place where they are all labeled, neatly wound up, and easy to access whenever you need them. Another option is to purchase a 3-inch binder so that your cords and chargers are easily portable. My tech binder includes zipper pouches that I've labeled—phone, computer, camera, tech accessories—and that contain my various cords. I also have one "crazy bag" for any cords I can't identify. Anytime I need a missing cord, I know it's probably there!

- ***Creating a charging station:*** Another thing I love is creating a dedicated place for charging my phone and iPad. There are charging stations available in stores and online like the one you see in the photograph, but you can also create your own. I have even purchased several inexpensive book storage boxes and then drilled small holes in the backs of them for my cords. Anytime I need to charge my phone, I open the box and tuck it away. You could do this with any beautiful storage box.

DO YOU NEED A DIGITAL DETOX?

Finally, I want to acknowledge that if you are truly feeling overwhelmed and don't think these tips and tools are enough, you might want to ask yourself if you need a "digital detox."

For many of us, technology is present in our lives from the time we wake up until we go to bed. That's why the idea of taking a break from technology has become such a popular and important trend.

A digital detox means creating time in your day or week to unplug and avoid checking your devices. If you work from home, then you may really be in need of a break, because you don't even get that small window of time in the car to take a break from your phone. Think about this: Our relationship with technology is often stronger than our relationships with human beings! That is why it is extremely important to periodically detox, to stay balanced.

To decide if you need a detox, answer these questions:

○ **DOES YOUR ATTENTION WANDER DURING CONVERSATIONS? DO YOU FEEL THE URGE TO CHECK YOUR PHONE—OR ACTUALLY DO IT—WHILE SOMEONE ELSE IS TALKING?**

○ **DO YOU FEEL DEPRESSED OR DOWN WHEN YOU SCROLL THROUGH SOCIAL MEDIA?**

○ **DO YOU HAVE TROUBLE FALLING ASLEEP OR GETTING GOOD-QUALITY SLEEP?**

○ **ARE YOUR EYES ITCHY, DRY, WATERY, OR BLURRY FROM SPENDING TOO MUCH TIME STARING AT SCREENS?**

○ **IS YOUR SMARTPHONE IN YOUR HAND MOST OF THE DAY?**

○ **CAN YOU WATCH TELEVISION WITHOUT HAVING YOUR PHONE, LAPTOP, OR TABLET AROUND?**

○ **DO YOU REACH FOR YOUR PHONE FIRST THING IN THE MORNING TO CHECK FOR TEXTS, E-MAILS, AND OTHER NOTIFICATIONS?**

○ **DO YOU LACK MENTAL CLARITY AND ALERTNESS, OR DO YOU HAVE A HARD TIME MAKING DECISIONS BECAUSE OF BRAIN FOG?**

○ **DO YOU USE YOUR DIGITAL DEVICE DURING MEALS?**

○ **DO OTHERS COMMENT ON YOUR ATTACHMENT TO YOUR PHONE?**

○ **DOES THE THOUGHT OF TURNING YOUR PHONE OFF OR PUTTING IT AWAY FOR A FEW HOURS STRESS YOU OUT?**

○ **ARE YOU SPENDING SO MUCH TIME ON YOUR DEVICES THAT YOU FIND YOURSELF LESS PHYSICALLY ACTIVE OR EVEN GAINING WEIGHT?**

If you answered yes to even a few of these, a digital detox could really be beneficial. If you said yes to five or more, then you should schedule a detox ASAP! You'll definitely feel better and see a change in your life after you do.

HOW TO DO A DIGITAL DETOX ▶ Now that you have done the assessment, it's time to detox!

Step 1: Prepare for your digital detox.

Step 2: Make a plan for dealing with withdrawal symptoms. How will you handle discomfort? Create a list of several options in your planner or in a beautiful motivational card that you write to yourself. Yes! Write to yourself using a pen or pencil.

Step 3: Set your digital detox dates. The sooner the better!

Step 4: Now that you have come so far, prevent yourself from going back to your old ways.

Make a list of benefits you've received from your detox:

- Mental health benefits
- Physical health benefits
- Relationship benefits, (e.g., having better relationships with friends and family)
- Benefits from having more free time
- Benefits that come from having an enhanced ability to focus and a longer attention span
- Productivity benefits
- Enhanced social skills from reconnecting with the "real" world

Use this digital detox assessment as an ongoing accountability tool.

CHAPTER FIVE

PLANNING AND SCHEDULING YOUR WORKDAY

Clients who come to me desperate for help with planning and scheduling often say they feel defeated. Many times, our first session is consumed by their frustrations about not being able to do it all. While they are venting, I often hear the same thing: "I feel like a hamster in a hamster wheel." Many of us are in such a frenzy to figure things out that we create multiple systems to try to stay on top of everything...when all we really need to do is have one source, one focus, one planning system.

We really only need one tool to keep us informed, on task, and on time. This could be a traditional planner, a digital planner, or a real-life personal assistant. You have options, but the key is to have only one tool. I had a client who had a different system for each of her tasks: She would constantly go to one spreadsheet to manage her projects and then another to manage her team. I thought the time she spent jumping from one spreadsheet to  the next impacted her ability to stay organized, so I immediately asked her to focus on just one thing. We then had fun deciding what that would be.

She decided that a digital planner would be the perfect assistant for her. Because she liked spreadsheets, I set her up with a single spreadsheet that logged everything she had to do by date and task. Her only job was to come to work and focus on that spreadsheet each day, knowing that it was set up to keep her from missing the mark on her tasks. It was such a simple fix that totally changed her workday for the better.

I'm a bit different. I've always been a fan of the physical planner, because it allows me to have all the information I need in one place, plus I can have it with me at all times, even when I don't have access to a computer. In this chapter, I will introduce you to all of your options and help you decide which one is best for you.

PHYSICAL PLANNERS

STEP ONE: *ASSESS*

If you're just starting out, I recommend getting a planner with a simple format that gives you plenty of room to write down all of your meetings and goals for each day in one place. Do some research by going to the store or online to see what kind of planner feels right to you. It might take you a few tries to find the one you like best. Remember to keep the size in mind. What feels most comfortable to you when writing? What will fit in your bag? You don't want a planner that is so big and cumbersome that you can't easily carry it around.

STEPS TWO & THREE: *DECLUTTER AND CLEAN*

If you have a system you are already using—be it another physical planner or notes on your computer or phone—spend some time gathering all of your information in one place. Rip out or delete any old information that's no longer needed or relevant. Focus on narrowing down your list to what needs to be done from this day forward, and then prepare to transfer that information into your new planner.

STEP 4: *ORGANIZE*

I like a planner that has tabs and dedicated areas for all of my information. When I'm setting up a planner for myself, my team, or my clients, it's important to me that it have at least these three sections:

- ***Master list:*** A master list is where you'll log all of your upcoming tasks and responsibilities and assign deadlines to each of them. Any time a new assignment arises, add it to the master list. You want to rest assured that you have kept track of everything you need to do, and having that information in one place is a great way to do that. No more worrying about forgetting that someone told you something or e-mailed you, asking you to do something! When a task arises, immediately add it to the master list.

- ***Calendar:*** Your calendar section is where you'll put all of your appointments, meetings, and calls. Just like with the master list, every time you schedule something (or it's scheduled for you), add it to your calendar immediately. That way, you'll know that it's always up to date and that you can glance at your calendar and know exactly what is coming up for you in the next week or month.

- **To-do list:** The to-do list is where you'll make a list of what needs to be done each day. Every morning, set aside time to plan your day. Open your planner and review your master list (with its accompanying deadlines) and your calendar. Add relevant information to your to-do list so you know exactly what needs to get done that day. Don't worry about future deadlines or other items that are farther out on the calendar! The goal of the to-do list is to help you focus and only spend time worrying about what your top priorities are for that day. I'll go into this more later on in this chapter.

OTHER TIPS FOR USING YOUR PLANNER ▶

- **Write in full sentences:** Often, when we are documenting an item, we will try to abbreviate, only to return to our planner later and not know what our notes actually mean. Write in full sentences so you have clarity!

- **Be specific:** It is important to be specific when documenting tasks on your planner. Instead of "Answer e-mail," write, "E-mail Susan." This saves time and keeps

you from relying on your memory, which is a longer process that can kill your productivity.

- **_Use verbs:_** When placing items on your to-do list and schedule, use verbs. This is a mental trick you can play on yourself to provide motivation. For example, instead of saying "Maria's proposal," make a note to "Write Maria's proposal."

- **_Leave your planner open:_** I like to keep my planner open on my desk all day as I work so I can mark off any to-dos as I go. It is so rewarding

- **_Acknowledge your accomplishments:_** Have a fun way to identify completed tasks in your planner. This can be another great way to motivate yourself! It may be as simple as highlighting a task when you complete it, placing a sticker next to the item, or adding a check mark.

- **_Add a brain dump page:_** Having a place in your planner to drop in all of your spontaneous ideas and thoughts is a great way to free your mind and document things that you want to reference later.

- **_Add a bookmark:_** In addition to using a planner with tabs, I like having a special bookmark so I can quickly open my planner to the current day. That helps me go right to what I need and not have to flip through past days' work.

- **_Only keep what you need:_** Keeping only the pages that you need in your planner will help you maintain it. Feel free to tear out old to-do lists as they are completed.

- **_Blank is not bad!:_** Just because you have remaining space in your calendar or planning pages does not mean you have to fill it! Only write down things you need to accomplish that day. Think of any open space as breathing room or a break in your schedule, and use it as such.

O

organize

OR·GA·NIZE | \ˈȯr·gə nīz'

ARRANGE INTO A STRUCTURED

WHOLE; ORDER.

Calendar

02.

TIP

Planners tend to be less expensive in March and April, when they are on clearance. That's when you can get a great deal on a 12- or 18-month planner.

STEP FIVE: *BEAUTIFY*

When you start diving into the world of planners, you will find that there is a huge selection of supplies available. It is important not to get drawn in and overload on supplies to the point where you've deviated from the very goal of a planner, which is to keep you on task.

- *Checkbox tool:* There are a variety of tools that make it easy for you to add checkboxes to your planner. They come in the form of stencils, punches, and stamps.

- *Washi tape:* Washi tape comes in a vast variety of colors, styles, and sizes, and it makes blocking out large amounts of time quick and easy. Washi tape also helps you color-code items on your page, and if you line the edges of your planner, you can use it as page markers or section dividers. You'll find a great selection of organizers for your washi tape. I find that I use the same washi tape all the time, so a simple tape dispenser makes for perfect storage.

- *Erasable pens:* Because things often change with your schedule and workload, an erasable pen is a great tool to have on hand.

- *Colored pens:* Colored pens are great for categorizing aspects of your schedule. If you manage a team, for example, you may have a certain color for each of your teammates or each task.

- *Highlighters:* A ruler is helpful when you are highlighting items or trying to review line items.

- **Stickers:** There are a variety of work-appropriate stickers that can bring fun and life to your planner.

- **Laminator:** Laminating certain resources in your planner is an excellent way to keep those pages clean and new. It also makes for a great dashboard for reminders.

- **Wite-Out:** Keep Wite-Out on hand to make needed corrections to your planner

DIGITAL PLANNERS AND CALENDARS

There are so many wonderful digital planning options these days! But before you sign up for one, remember the golden rule of planning: Keep it simple. Many online tools have a *lot* of features, and learning how to use them all can send you down a rabbit hole.

One way to keep it simple is to create a spreadsheet with tabs, just like the tabs you would have in a physical planner. Keep your master list in one dedicated tab and your daily to-do list in another.

In terms of digital calendars, I recommend using a calendar system connected to your e-mail, because any appointments or invitations will automatically be added.

Here are a few services worth looking into if you opt for a digital planner.

- **Evernote:** A note-taking tool, Evernote allows you to keep your tasks, calendar, and to-do list in one place that will also sync up across all of your devices. That way, when you add a note to your phone, it will show up on Evernote when you open your laptop. You can also access the information on your device when Wi-Fi is not available.

- **Any.do:** Any.do is an award-winning smart assistant that allows you to have a calendar, tasks, lists, and reminders in one place. It also syncs across devices.

- **Trello, Airtable, Asana:** These are just a few examples of the many online platforms available for scheduling and planning across team members or departments. They are helpful when you need to share your schedule and plan with others. If you go this route, I recommend having one dedicated tech-savvy person on your team to help set this up to make it easier for everyone.

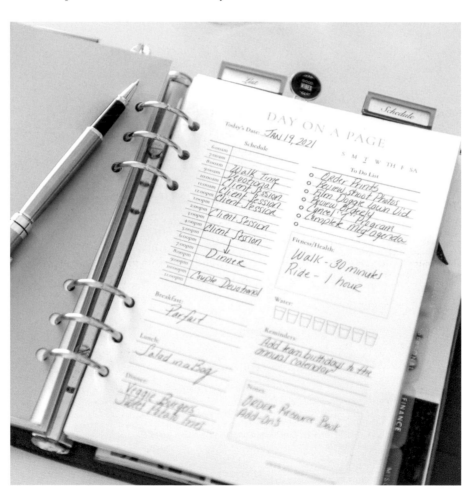

HOW TO PRIORITIZE YOUR DAY

Take 15 minutes at the start of your day to write out your schedule. Doing so is more productive than trying to plan in advance: Because you are scheduling in real time, you can focus on the present moment. Don't check e-mails, take calls, or engage with others during this time. Grab a cup of coffee or tea and think of it as an appointment with yourself.

SET YOUR TOP THREE DAILY GOALS ▸ When working out your schedule for the day, set your top three (reasonable) goals. Quality beats quantity every time. If you set three obtainable goals each day, it will be easier to motivate yourself, because you won't have a long, scary list. It also makes your list more achievable, which will leave you with a sense of accomplishment at the end of the day. Over the course of a workweek, three daily goals turn into 15 completed goals!

BREAK DOWN YOUR GOALS ▸ When you're looking at your master list, some of the tasks might feel daunting, because you know there is a lot of work to be done. That is when you need to break them down into smaller goals that are easier to accomplish each day. When planning your day, put those smaller goals on your to-do list throughout the week so that by the end of the week or month, the bigger goal will be completed.

SET ASIDE FOCUS TIME ▸ Just as I want you to take 15 minutes of uninterrupted time each morning to write your to-do list, I want you to create a window within your day in which you are not interrupted, not taking calls, and not checking e-mails. This is when you can really focus on your top three tasks and make sure nothing is distracting you from getting them done.

CREATE ROUTINES ▸ You might do certain tasks every day. Have set times and routines for these tasks so you are able to calculate the amount of time they will take every day.

COLOR-CODE ▸ Color-coding your to-do list is a great way to quickly identify and maintain items in your planner. It is also a great way to identify how long a task may take. In other words, color-coding will help you prioritize! For example, I like to use different-colored highlighters or washi tape to mark the time allotted for my tasks:

- *Yellow*: Tasks that take 15 minutes or less
- *Green*: Tasks that take less than 1 hour
- *Orange*: Tasks that take over 2 hours

PLAN FULL CIRCLE ▸ When planning out tasks, start with your most important commitments, but also include light-minded/fun things you have going on at work, such as lunch breaks or a coworker's birthday celebration. This will provide a good balance to your schedule and keep it from feeling so heavy.

DON'T FORGET "ME TIME" ▸ It is important to think about *yourself* during the planning process! Schedule times to step away, have lunch, or read a few pages of your favorite novel. It is important to give yourself those refresher moments; put them on your schedule to remind yourself to take that time.

EVALUATE YOUR DAY ▸ At the end of the day, evaluate how your day went so you can make any necessary adjustments. Ask yourself, *How could I have improved my day or better used my time?*

One thing that often gets in the way of productivity and staying on schedule is time spent stressing about things going on at home. That's why I think it's important not to ignore home life while you're at work. Instead, build check-ins into your schedule so you can stay connected throughout the day.

- **CALL YOUR FAMILY.** Make it a routine to call your spouse and children during your breaks. Simply call to say, "I love you" or "I hope your day is going great." Try not to run down the to-do list for the evening or complain about work. The call should be fun and uplifting.

- **RECORD OR SEND A QUICK VIDEO.** Record a video clip sharing part of your day, such as showing them what you are having for lunch or how you just cleaned off your desk. If you don't love recording yourself, send them a funny YouTube video or something that will make them smile instead. These little connections throughout the day can make you and your family feel as though you are a part of each other's day.

- **COORDINATE TIME WITH DAY-CARE PROVIDERS.** Ask your day-care provider if they would be willing and able to use an app to allow you to connect with your child during the day or observe them playing.

- **SHOW YOUR PET SOME LOVE.** If you feel guilty about leaving your pets, think about investing in a Wi-Fi interactive pet camera with a treat dispenser, such as Furbo. This will allow you to check on your pet and let them hear your voice right from your mobile phone, plus it also allows you to give them a treat. This investment can bring you years of comfort while at work and alleviate your pet's separation anxiety.

- **TAKE A PERSONAL DAY AND SPEND IT WITH YOUR CHILDREN OR YOUR PARTNER.** Take a day off to do something you typically do not have time to do during a normal workweek, such as riding bikes together or going to the mall. If you are unable to take a full day off from work, you can pick your children up from school early or dedicate a weekend to being a "fun weekend" to catch up on quality time.

CHAPTER SIX

WORKING WELL ON A TEAM

I'll admit it: Sometimes I drive my employees crazy! As the head of the company and someone with a creative brain, my mind is constantly brainstorming new ideas and ways to grow our business.

For the longest time, I would simply share my ideas with my employees whenever inspiration struck. That was good for me, but it was bad for them, because they couldn't keep the ideas organized or ever get around to executing them. After enough griping, I realized I needed to create a system to help my team manage *me*. My solution: The "Nikki Do" list.

Whenever anyone has joined my team, I have always created a customized planner for them that has dedicated spaces for their master list, calendar, to-do list, and meeting and client notes. Now, I also include the "Nikki Do" list as its own separate tab. The list is a space they can quickly turn to anytime I share a new idea. They write all of the new ideas in one place, and they can refer back to it during meetings or whenever we are talking about new business or ideas.

The list has become a tool that relieves my team's stress, because they have one place where they can keep all of my ideas. It's also made *my* life easier, because now they can remind me of my ideas during our meetings. It gives my team structure for keeping track of new ideas and reassures me that nothing is slipping through the cracks.

Working on a team—whether in the same space or remotely—is rewarding, but it's also challenging at times. Everyone has their own way of doing things, and even though you can spend a lot of time planning out your workspace and workday, sometimes the only thing you can fit into your day is dealing with other people's distractions or priorities.

This chapter is focused on tools I've used to work better with others. Co-workers can give us camaraderie and a shared sense of purpose, and they are often the people we interact with the most during the week. That means we need to learn how to work together effectively!

Because teams consist of different personalities, ideas, and work styles, it is important to have a unified front when it comes to a company's organizational structure. If every football player gets onto the field and does what they think is best as an individual, the team will inevitably lose the game. Successful teams have organized methods of getting work done and great ways to communicate. In my work life, I use several essential tools to make sure my team and I are on the same page. These tips are great for managers to implement, but even if you aren't the boss, I still encourage you to suggest these tools as ways to improve collaboration with your teammates.

CREATE A SHARED MISSION AND VISION

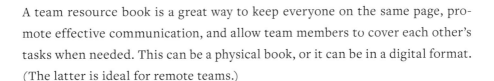

A team resource book is a great way to keep everyone on the same page, promote effective communication, and allow team members to cover each other's tasks when needed. This can be a physical book, or it can be in a digital format. (The latter is ideal for remote teams.)

WHAT IS IN A TEAM RESOURCE BOOK ▸

- ***Mission and vision statement:*** The first things that should be included are the company's mission and vision statements, as these are the guiding force behind all tasks that team members will be focusing on. These documents also serve as motivation for the team, because they are constantly reminded of what they are working toward.

- ***Protocols/procedures:*** Protocols and procedures for the processes of the company should be outlined in the resource book so every team member can understand and easily reference the flow of a given process. One of the best ways to organize this is in a flowchart that shows the entire process for any given task. This keeps everyone on the same page and clearly identifies any potential issues within a process.

- ***Team fact sheet:*** A one-page team fact sheet is a great tool to add to your team resource book. This serves as a quick reference for the entire team. It contains all team members' names and contact numbers; all of the online resources that team members access each day, such as websites; team members' social media profiles for the company; conference call numbers; and the company's telephone number and address. It is essentially one sheet that the team can easily reference for their basic everyday information.

- **The team:** Lastly, share the team. Include a photo of each team member, their title, and a fun fact. This helps with work relations.

BUILD MORALE AND CAMARADERIE

Many teams work remotely, and this can cause a team to become detached, disorganized, and focused only on their individual role rather than the team's as a whole. This can affect the success of the team. Create a designated place to keep up with your team and build morale and camaraderie. This can take the form of an informal weekly e-mail newsletter or a shared channel on a communication tool like Slack. Use this dedicated space to share team members' successes and personal celebrations as well as inspirations, fun facts, and simple reminders. Doing so will help the team feel connected and cohesive.

MANAGE PROJECTS EFFECTIVELY

When working on a team, tasks often need to be divided among team members according to each person's skill set and role within the organization. Although everyone has their individual tasks, they should all come together to form one completed goal. But how do coworkers manage a variety of tasks as a team? By having one project management tool!

There are many management tools on the market, including Trello, Airtable, and Asana, as mentioned in Chapter 5. Many programs are free, with paid options also available. They all have helpful features, but that does not always translate to bringing order to your team. Why? Because these  tools require people to use them, and not everyone is going to buy into using such programs, especially if they are not very tech savvy.

My remedy is to keep things simple! Even if a program has an abundance of tools, don't get drawn into using all of the options from the start, as that can hinder productivity and increase confusion. By starting with the basics, team members give themselves the opportunity to grow into their system.

CREATE A WORK BASE ▶ No matter what program you choose, I recommend setting up a work base for yourself where your team members can view your work tasks, deadlines for the tasks, details of the tasks, the status of the tasks, and any notes. This one centralized spreadsheet lists what everyone should be working on.

WHAT ARE THE BENEFITS? ▶

- Team members can easily cover each other when needed and see where a team member is on a task.

- Team leaders can easily oversee team workloads.

- Deadlines are clearly defined and less likely to be missed.

- It provides a structure that allows each team member to maximize their productivity.

Work Base Example

BARBARA'S WORK BASE

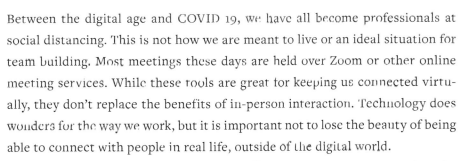

☐	▦ SUSPENSE DATE ⌄	☰ TASK ⌄	☰ TASK DETAILS ⌄	☰ STATUS ⌄	☰ NOTES ⌄
1	4/29/2021	Mail product FLEX product samples		PENDING	
2	4/29/2021	Update team computers		PENDING	
3	4/29/2021	Send estimates to vendor		COMPLETED	
4	4/29/2021	Create PR proposal		APPROVED	
5	4/30/2021	Schedule meeting w/marketing team	Purpose: To discuss the FLEX project	PENDING	
6	4/30/2021	Send team newsletter		PENDING	
7	4/30/2021	Run monthly reports		PENDING	
8	4/30/2021	Research ABC company		PENDING	

MAKE VIRTUAL MEETINGS TANGIBLE

Between the digital age and COVID 19, we have all become professionals at social distancing. This is not how we are meant to live or an ideal situation for team building. Most meetings these days are held over Zoom or other online meeting services. While these tools are great for keeping us connected virtually, they don't replace the benefits of in-person interaction. Technology does wonders for the way we work, but it is important not to lose the beauty of being able to connect with people in real life, outside of the digital world.

If your team does a lot of work virtually, surprise your team members by sending them something tangible in the mail prior to your meeting. This can be a coffee gift card, a fun notepad, or cute Post-it notes. Think about anything you can do to connect with your team members in a concrete way. It's a great way to build morale and incorporate fun into the workplace!

DEALING WITH A NEGATIVE COWORKER

You can wake up in the best mood in the world, only to have it crushed by a negative coworker the instant you walk into the office. The people we surround ourselves with at work often have a big impact on our ability to be happy there. Fostering positive relationships in the workplace—with both your coworkers and supervisors—is so important!

If you are struggling in this area, start by identifying the problems within your workplace that are causing stress for you and perhaps for others. You may not be able to change the actions of a coworker, but you can change how you allow them to affect you. Here are a few tips to assist you in dealing with a toxic coworker.

HAVE A CONVERSATION ▸ Communicating is an essential first step when having a dispute with a coworker. Before going to your supervisor, start by speaking directly with the individual. This will build trust and respect, even if you disagree on an issue. Offer to take them to lunch or out for a cup of coffee. Start the conversation on a positive note prior to addressing the issue. You may find that you can easily resolve the issue—and you just may gain a new friend.

HAVE AN EXIT STRATEGY ▸ Having an exit strategy when you're in a situation with a difficult coworker can keep your stress level down and defuse the situation. Pretending you have an urgent task or taking a fake call can get you away from a toxic encounter with a teammate.

TURN A NEGATIVE INTO A POSITIVE ▸ Someone once gave me great advice on how to deal with a negative coworker. Instead of being frustrated, think of yourself as a scientist placed within the organization to research a negative specimen called "coworker." Keep a little notebook to keep track of all the negative encounters. This may also be helpful if you go to HR in the future.

DON'T LET TOXIC COWORKERS INVADE YOUR THOUGHTS ▸ If you continue to worry about a negative conversation with a coworker at home, you are allowing them to bring toxicity into your personal life and possibly affect you and your family's happiness. If you find yourself constantly worrying at home about a situation at work, it is time to take action and flip your thoughts! Find a way to create some fun: Call a girlfriend and talk about something not work related, speed-clean the house, or go for a run or walk.

KEEP A SENSE OF HUMOR ▸ Any situation is easier if you can laugh about it. You may be able to find some entertainment value in the issue with your coworker.

EXPRESS GRATITUDE FOR YOUR COWORKERS

Teams need to work together to maintain a work-life balance as much as possible. When you see that a team member is struggling, try these tips to give them a reset.

- Place a card on their desk with a funny (but appropriate) joke.

- E-mail them a gift card to their favorite coffee shop.

- Schedule a lunch date (in person or virtual) with them and do not talk about work.

- Enjoy some laugh therapy together. Send your coworker a funny (work-appropriate) meme or YouTube.

CHAPTER SEVEN

STAYING ORGANIZED
AROUND THE OFFICE

One of my most rewarding client projects was redecorating a company break room.

A break room is meant to be a place where you can relax and recharge during your workday, where you can take a few minutes to yourself and maybe have a cup of coffee or a delicious lunch. The reality, though, is that many break rooms are clutter pits, filled with dirty dishes, expired food, and items employees have brought from home and dumped there for their coworkers. Day-old banana bread, anyone?

This client's break room was so cluttered that the client avoided it altogether. But when I assessed the space, I saw so much potential! I knew it could become a place where team members could get a great start to their workday as well as sneak off to for a quick boost when their eyes got heavy in the afternoon.

The first mission was to close down the company's version of Goodwill. I removed all of the excessive toasters, coffee mugs, coffee makers, and dishes, placing them on the table in their conference room. Everyone had a day to shop the table and take anything home they wanted, and then the rest was off to the real Goodwill.

Because this office was home to a small team, I knew it would be important to identify personal areas in the break room. That would keep everyone accountable for their space: If anyone was not keeping their area tidy, it would be apparent to everyone else. I set up bins for everyone's personal food items in the cabinets as well as in the fridge. I also added motivational signage to encourage the team to tidy up as they used the space.

In the end, everything had its own place. The final touch was to add not only beautiful flowers to the space but also special features, such as a fruit bin in the fridge that allowed them to infuse their water in the afternoon. I also placed water glasses in the fridge so they would have chilled glasses to drink from—an extra-special touch. The break room had become a truly special place to come for a break instead of a place to break away *from*!

If you work in an office and the shared spaces are not enhancing your team's productivity, I encourage you to discuss this with your supervisor—or implement changes if you are in charge. Bring suggestions to the conversation and impress your supervisor by drawing out a floor plan or researching some best practices. In the end, every company wants to foster growth and productivity. The suggestions in this chapter are recommendations I have from my own experience running a small business. If you work in a bigger corporate environment, I understand that having an influence on these shared spaces may be more difficult, but I hope you still learn some new approaches that you can try to bring to your office. And if you work at home, you might still find some of these tips helpful for when you have to navigate sharing common spaces (like your kitchen or living room) during your workday.

CUBICLES AND OPEN WORKSPACES

If you don't have the benefit of having your own office, where you can close the door and get complete privacy and quiet, then you have to adapt your workspace, knowing that distractions from others are a possibility.

If your office has cubicles, they can provide some level of privacy, but they still don't block out noise as well as they could: Partitions block the view of others, not the sound of their voices. Your teammates can hear all of your calls, and you can hear all of theirs.

Here are some ways to cope.

NOISE TIPS ▶

- Use earbuds or noise-cancelling headphones.
- Place items such as plants or lamps in front of gaps within the cubicle

walls or anywhere you need to create a barrier from distractions.

- Use sound-absorbing plants, such as ferns, peace lilies, or fiddle leaf figs.

- Adjust your seating so you face the side with less noise.

- If you need to make phone calls, you should go to a private area if you do not want to be overheard.

Smells can also be an issue with cubicles or open workspaces, especially when your work neighbor decides to have lunch at their desk or puts on an additional layer of perfume. This can be a big distraction and also very frustrating.

SMELL TIPS ▸

- Use an aromatherapy diffuser in your space.

- Brew a cup of mint tea. Simply having mint tea on your desk—even if you are not going to drink it—makes the space smell fresh!

- Plants purify the area and can be a good resource to combat smells.

- A few times a week at the end of the day, spray all textile surfaces— your chair, fabric cubicle walls—with linen spray.

- Sprinkle baking soda in your trash can.

- Add a few drops of essential oil to your light bulb when it's cold and not in use. The next time you turn it on, the heat will warm the oil and diffuse the scent in your space.

PRIVACY TIPS ▸ If your desk is visible to others, having inbox covers like we discussed earlier can be a great way to conceal your workload and keep your desk area looking minimalistic and clean. By simply laminating an attractive sheet of paper and placing it on top of any paperwork, it immediately removes documents from the view of prying eyes.

KEEP YOUR AREA SANITIZED ▸ Note that if you share desk space with others, it's important to keep your area sanitized. Put together a small kit with sanitizer, disinfectant, gloves, and a mask. Wipe down your phone and work area several times a day.

RECEPTION AREA

A reception desk is another area that is visible and accessible to almost everyone in the office. It's also often the first thing someone sees when they enter the office, so it's critical to make it a welcoming environment for both guests and the receptionist. If you work in a reception area or manage an office that has one, here are some tips for bringing more order to your space.

- Does your reception area reflect the vibe and professionalism of the office? You want to create a mood and experience that is inviting the second someone walks through your doors.

- You will be taking calls and juggling office tasks, and you don't want your work cluttering up your desk. A special binder with a beautiful cover can serve as a place to take messages and add sticky notes yet conceal them from anyone who walks up to the desk.

- Get a desk caddy and attractive desk accessories. Put your notebooks, pens, and staplers on the caddy so they are neatly organized on your desk.

- Keep fresh flowers on your desk, light a candle, or keep a candy bowl—anything to make it a pleasant experience.

CONFERENCE ROOM

The conference room is one of the most important spaces in an office. It's where many of the company secrets are held and decisions are made. It is a space that brings a team together to focus and be creative. It's also where we

celebrate business successes, individual team member accomplishments, and more. The conference room holds many important memories for a company. Because it's a fairly important space, it's essential to make sure it stays clean, well organized, and equipped with just what the team needs to focus and shine!

CONFERENCE TABLE ▸ The focal point of most meeting spaces is the conference room table. This is the tool that brings a team together to focus, brainstorm, and execute company goals. Here are some things to consider when it comes to the function of the table.

- *Shape:* The shape of a conference room table contributes to the experience the team members have when in the space together. Rectangular tables emphasize the leader sitting at either end, while tables without sharp corners (like an oval or round table) create a more comfortable environment for your team.

- *Function:* Because the conference room table is the hub of the space, how it functions is crucial. To bring maximum function to your conference room table, include phone stands at each chair. Another idea is to choose a table with built-in storage, which can be a great space saver in a small office.

- *Technology:* Plugs and USB ports are great tools to have available on the conference table. If your table does not already have these, you can install a connectivity box for them. This is a simple fix for a huge burst of function! If you do not want to alter the furniture, you can get a tabletop version that does not require any installation.

CHAIRS ▸ Because a variety of people will be sitting in them, conference room chairs must be adjustable and easy to move around. There are five things to consider when choosing the right chair.

- *Aesthetics:* Do the chairs look nice in the conference room? Do they match the other décor?

- *Durability:* Will they hold up over time? Remember, these chairs will be used many times by many people.

- *Mobility:* Are they easy to move around?

- *Adjustability:* Are the chairs adjustable so everyone can make the height of their chair convenient for them?

- *Comfort:* Are the chairs comfortable, particularly for sitting in during long meetings?

THE ROOM ▸ The room itself should be inviting as well as functional, and it should be one of the most minimalist spaces within an office. It is also im-

portant to make sure that presentation tools, such as podiums, monitors, and whiteboards, don't disrupt the flow of the space or create clutter. Here are a few tips to keep in mind.

- Utilize vertical space. Hang monitors and whiteboards on the wall, and consider retractable monitors and whiteboards if possible.

- Incorporate acrylic and glass podiums and whiteboards to make the space feel more open.

- Use a whiteboard or chalkboard paint to create walls and/or tables that can be written on.

- Add a Bluetooth speaker to the conference room speaker. This will enhance the sound quality when meeting with remote team members/people.

- Add a small bowl of candy to the table. This is a great go-to when people need a little pep during brainstorming sessions.

- Presentation covers are a great addition to a conference table, plus they conceal paper clutter, leaving the table looking more open and organized.

- A nice centerpiece can be a great way to bring inspiration to the conference table. But make sure it is not distracting and does not obstruct any team member's view. Plants bring life to a space and can be a great option.

THE BEVERAGE STATION ▸ A beverage station is a wonderful amenity to add to your meeting space. Here is a simple checklist of some items to include.

- ○ **COFFEE MAKER**
- ○ **COFFEE CUPS**
- ○ **COFFEE / TEA**
- ○ **BOTTLED WATER**
- ○ **CREAMER, SUGAR, AND SUGAR SUBSTITUTES**
- ○ **COFFEE STIRRERS**
- ○ **NAPKINS**
- ○ **TRASH CAN**

KITCHEN / BREAK ROOM

As I mentioned in the opening of this chapter, the company break room can sometimes become one of the most difficult rooms to maintain, because everyone on staff is trafficking in and out of it throughout the day and using it to make coffee, bring in food from home, make food, or toss food. Think about the kitchen in your home and how challenging it can be to keep it tidy and the sink free of dishes! That's why it's essential to create an organized system for everyone to follow. Here are some tips to expand on the ones I mentioned earlier.

DECLUTTER ▸ Start by going into the break room and throwing out any old food, either on the counters or in the fridge. This should become part of your cleaning schedule. Before you can organize your break room, you need to clear out anything that's been lingering in there for too long. Also take any magnets off the fridge and remove any other items that have collected in the room but aren't adding any value or aesthetic appeal.

REPLACE MISMATCHED COFFEE MUGS WITH STYLISH ONES ▸

Far too often, break rooms become dumping grounds for coffee mugs that coworkers have gotten for free somewhere. While functional, these mugs are often mismatched and don't look good in the office. Clean those out of the cabinets and donate them and replace them with some from a same set.

ORGANIZE THE CABINETS AND FRIDGE ▸

Once you've tossed out what's no longer needed, it's time to create specialized areas for what you keep. In the fridge, use bins to organize water bottles and soda cans. If you have a small team, give each person a dedicated space in the fridge for their lunch

and a spot in the cabinets for their snacks. That way, you know what belongs to whom. Label the shelves in the cabinets so everyone will know where coffee pods, tea, and everything else should go. Move any appliances or lesser-used items to the top shelves and more frequently used items within reach.

ESTABLISH A COFFEE STATION ▸ This is usually the most used space in a break room, so it's important to keep it clean and orderly. Use small organizer bins to hold creamers, sugar packets, and stirrers. If you have a Keurig or similar coffee maker, get a nice carousel or drawer to house your coffee pods.

SET UP A SNACK JAR OR DRAWER ▸ Fill it with individual-serving cracker packs, oatmeal, nutrition bars, and small candies—anything someone can easily grab and go. If using a drawer, be sure to put these snacks in dividers or bins so they aren't scattered throughout.

CREATE A CLEANING SCHEDULE ▸ If your company doesn't have outside cleaning help, then you need to establish a rotating schedule where everyone does their part, making sure dishes end up in the dishwasher at the end of the day and old food gets tossed at the end of the week. Keep basic cleaning supplies and extra paper towels neatly organized under the sink.

SUPPLY ROOM

Office supplies can become a huge clutter problem in an office if they are not managed properly. The supply room often ends up being the "junk room," because it's usually for employees only and not seen by visitors. Between copier paper, paper clips, pens, and a host of other small items, a company can lose revenue from not having an organized system in place to maintain the supply cabinet. Here are some tips to regulate the cabinet.

LIMIT ACCESS ▸ Limiting access to the supply cabinet can really help keep it in order. The fewer hands that physically engage with the cabinet, the better your chances of keeping it organized. Choose one team member—or maybe a few—to be the gatekeeper for the cabinet. Limit access to only them, and have them be responsible for distributing supplies. Another option is to create a log for employees and hang it in the supply cabinet.

HAVE AN OFFICE SUPPLY PURGE PARTY ▸ Have everyone purge their desk of any supplies they are not using and either exchange them or toss them. You can make these supply purge parties a monthly event.

CREATE CATEGORIES ▸ Sort supplies by grouping like items together and giving each group its own dedicated place. Label these areas so they are clearly defined and you can remember where everything goes. Use bins to hold smaller items, such as paper clips and pens.

USE WHAT YOU HAVE ▸ Before buying new office supplies, encourage employees to use what is on hand. This prevents waste.

USE AUTOMATION ▸ Set up an automated ordering system to receive supplies. This is a great way to put management of the office supply cabinet on

TIP

If you have large inventory items, such as boxes and supplies, think about moving them off-site so they don't disrupt the workable office space. Set up the storage grocery-store style so it is easy to access the items.

autopilot. Amazon and Staples are great resources for this.

KEEP AN INVENTORY LOG ▸ Having an inventory log is the best way to keep track of office supplies. There are several free inventory templates online that will help you with this process, or you can use a platform such as SOS Inventory, Sortly, or Delivrd. Depending on the quantity of supplies you have, a scanning system may be worth the small investment. Keep in mind that an inventory log only works if it is maintained.

BATHROOM

If there is one space that should be extremely clean and organized within an office, it is the bathroom. But because bathroom maintenance varies, your experience can vary. Some companies are larger and have cleaning teams that monitor and keep the bathroom cleaned throughout the day, which is a luxury. A smaller business, such as a dentist's office or small retail store, may rely on their team to keep the bathroom orderly. Regardless if your workplace is in a small building or large office complex—or even a home office—the bathroom needs to be comfortable for both men and women.

Use this guide to take inventory and make sure you have all the essentials.

BATHROOM INVENTORY CHECKLIST ▸

- ○ **SOAP DISPENSER AND HAND SANITIZER**
- ○ **CLEANERS**
- ○ **TOILET SEAT COVERS**
- ○ **SPARE TOILET PAPER**
- ○ **TRASH CAN/TRASH BAGS**

PLEASE

Wash

YOUR HANDS

○ **PAPER TOWELS OR HAND DRYER**

○ **CLEANING SCHEDULE**

○ **TEAM SURVIVAL KIT**

○ **BATHROOM SIGNAGE**

○ **FRESHENING SPRAY**

○ **MIRRORS**

○ **PLUNGER**

○ **TOILET BOWL CLEANER**

Get rid of anything that isn't on the inventory list or doesn't belong in the bathroom, and then give it a thorough cleaning. Along with this initial cleaning, it is important to set up a cleaning schedule for maintaining the bathroom.

BATHROOM CLEANING CHECKLIST ▶

- ○ **DUST**
- ○ **SWEEP**
- ○ **EMPTY TRASH**
- ○ **REFILL PRODUCTS (SOAP, HAND SANITIZER, PAPER TOWELS)**
- ○ **CLEAN TOILETS AND URINALS**
- ○ **CLEAN SINKS, MIRRORS, AND COUNTERTOPS**
- ○ **CLEAN WALLS AND FIXTURES**
- ○ **MOP FLOOR**
- ○ **PUT UP "WET FLOOR" SIGN**

ORGANIZE ▶ When it comes to organizing the office bathroom, it's best to keep things simple and visible so the entire team and all guests can clearly see all the amenities and directives. Here are some tips to help bring beautiful order to your office bathroom:

- Use clear organizers under the sink to store products so they can be found easily.

- Use vertical space to store items such as trash bags (nicely disguised in a basket on the shelf).

- Cosmetic bags are great for concealing sensitive items, such as sanitary napkins, in a drawer or under a cabinet.

- Magazine holders are great organizers under the sink, as they can obscure unsightly pipes and maximize the space.

- Tension rods are a great tool to place under cabinets to hang bottled cleaning items.

- To save every inch of space in the bathroom, use toilet brushes designed to fit in the corner behind the toilet.

TIP

Keep the look of all bathroom signage cohesive to prevent a cluttered appearance within the space. Use signs to communicate in a kind way and be careful of the tone. It is important to keep signs informative but courteous! Refrain from demanding words, such as "Don't," and instead say, "Please..." Also, use wording that makes each team member feel as if it were *their* space: "This is your bathroom. Please keep it clean." Your signage should reflect your company's brand, particularly if clients and/or visitors will be using the bathroom.

- Skinny garbage cans save space in a bathroom, because they can fit between a toilet and a wall or cabinet.

- A full-length mirror in the bathroom allows team members and guests to quickly check their outfits before leaving the bathroom. As a bonus, some wall-mounted mirrors include built-in storage.

BEAUTIFY ▸

- Incorporating an audio system into the bathroom and playing music is a nice touch. A sound machine can be another good option.

- Automatic air fresheners are a great addition to an office bathroom.

- Adding a simple plant can bring beauty to an often sterile environment.

- Put up attractive artwork.

- An appealing paint color can bring life to a bathroom.

OFFICE SURVIVAL KIT

An office survival kit can be a great resource for team members and is essential in any office. This can be a kit that is kept in the bathroom under the sink, neatly displayed on the counter, or even mounted to the wall to save space. Here's what to include.

- SPARE TOOTHBRUSHES
- DENTAL FLOSS
- TOOTHPASTE
- SHOUT WIPES
- LINT ROLLER
- SANITARY NAPKINS AND WIPES
- FINGERNAIL POLISH REMOVER
- NEUTRAL AND CLEAR NAIL POLISH
- NAIL FILE
- DEODORANT WIPES
- EYE DROPS
- ASPIRIN
- SEWING KIT
- FLAT IRON
- HAIR SPRAY

8

CHAPTER EIGHT

WORKING FROM HOME
AND ON THE GO

The old song "Wherever I Lay My Hat (That's My Home)" by Marvin Gaye should be the theme song for us these days as it relates to our work lives! After all, many of us find ourselves working in so many different environments: in the office, at home, in our cars, in a coffee shop, on a plane. If you're not organized, working remotely or on the go can be very stressful.

I have a client who now works seamlessly from home, the corporate office, *and* on the go, because we worked together to create a system that allows her office to move as she moves. It was a simple fix to not only create a motivating and inspiring workspace at all three locations but make all of her functional items mobile as well.

If you frequently work in different places, you need to take many special considerations into account to make sure your new environments don't disrupt your work. This chapter will cover some of the systems I like to put in place whenever I'm working outside the office.

WORKING FROM HOME

It is important to create a beautiful desk area in your home—a dedicated space where you can work *and* leave work behind each day. I know everyone's home setup is different, but if at all possible, avoid having your work area in your bedroom, which should be reserved for rest. You don't want to be staring at your work across the room as you're trying to fall asleep. If you don't have space for a dedicated office, try to integrate your work area into another room in your home to give it a dual purpose. For example, if you are a new mom, create a work area in the nursery that coordinates with the nursery décor. Here are some other ideas.

- *Use an armoire as your office.* Making over an armoire can be the perfect solution for a home office. Place a pegboard on the back wall of the

interior of the armoire to hold all of your supplies, and then install a roll-out tabletop for your desk. Use any shelves in the armoire for your printer or other office tools.

- *Make a closet into an office.* A closet is a wonderful space to transition into an office. By simply adding a desk to the closet or DIY'ing a table in the space, you can create a functional workspace. Use pegboards or shelving to house your items.

- *Use a folding screen.* Folding screens can be an attractive way to create division within a space in your home for your office. It also makes a great backdrop for your conference calls.

TECH CONSIDERATIONS ▶

- *Invest in reliable internet service.* When you are trying to work from home, having a bad internet connection is extremely frustrating—and unproductive. If your connection is not the best, think about upgrading the level of service you're getting from your provider.

- *Buy a good surge protector.* Be sure to use a surge protector for your computer and printer. There is a big difference between a power strip and a surge protector! Power strips are less expensive, multi-outlet strips that simply allow you to have additional outlets for convenience but do not offer any real protection. Surge protectors, on the other hand, offer protection against power and voltage spikes.

- *Check the VPN.* Working remotely is a security risk when it comes to data on your computer. Be sure your company or you have set up a VPN (virtual private network), which creates a secure tunnel between your off-site office IT infrastructure and your home.

WORK-LIFE BALANCE AT HOME ▸ When you are working from home, it's important to create boundaries so that work doesn't spill over into your family time or time for relaxation. It's also important to make efforts to get into "work mode" at home.

- *Maintain regular work hours.* When working from home or anywhere outside the office, create regular work hours. You'll still have bound- aries, helping create a better balance between work life and home life. Doing so will bring stability not only to the com- pany you work for but also, more important, to your family and home life.

- *Get dressed.* Getting dressed in the morning is huge for pro- ductivity. That's how you set the tone for your day.

- *Set ground rules with fami- ly and friends.* Be sure to let friends and family know that you are working from home, and announce what your work schedule is. This will minimize disruptions. You can even create a sign for your home office door that lets them know when you are in meetings or unavailable.

- **Schedule breaks.** Be sure to schedule breaks. You tend to lose time when you are working alone at home. Set aside time for small breaks throughout the day to rejuvenate yourself.

- **Don't forget to socialize.** It can be lonely working from home. Schedule a Zoom lunch date with a team member to stay socially connected.

WORKING FROM A COFFEE SHOP

Do your research! Some coffee shops are more work friendly than others. Find a space that provides your desired work environment; free Wi-Fi and easy access to power strips are good indicators. Here are some more tips.

- When working from a coffee shop, timing is everything. Try not to work during their busiest times. Trying to get work done during the morning rush can be a bit distracting. Coffeehouses are packed as people run in to get their first cup of joe.

- Come with all of your equipment fully charged in case you can't snag a seat next to an outlet.

- Have a headset with you so you can stay focused and minimize distractions.

- Be friendly! If you plan to utilize the coffee shop as an ongoing work spot, be friendly to the staff. That can bring you nothing but work perks!

- You can also use the coffeehouse as a great networking opportunity. Take some time away from your headset to connect with others who are working there.

WORKING FROM YOUR CAR

Now that so many people are working from home, the car has turned into a mini conference room when you need to sneak away from the kids to have a little peace and quiet for a meeting. Working from your car can also be a great getaway whenever you need a little change of environment. Besides, many people have to be in transit most of the day for their jobs. But keep the following things in mind.

- Before working in your car, make sure you know the coverage areas for your cellular and Wi-Fi service. You may need to invest in a Wi-Fi booster. You can also plan your workload so that most of the work you do in your car is off-line.

- Invest in a power inverter to give yourself needed outlets for your laptop, phone, and other tech items.

- Invest in a car mount for your phone or tablet. This will free up space and make it easier to work in such a small space.

- A lap or wheel desk is a great option for working in your car. Police officers work in their cars daily and have great desk systems. You may want to invest in a police-spec car desk.

- A small shower caddy with suction cups makes a great holder for pens and sticky notes while working in your car.

- Be sure to position your laptop and tech items away from the sun.

- Connect to your car's Bluetooth for conference calls or use a Bluetooth headset.

- The great thing about working in your car is that you can control your environment. Finding a beautiful park or lakefront where you can park can make working from your car more enjoyable.

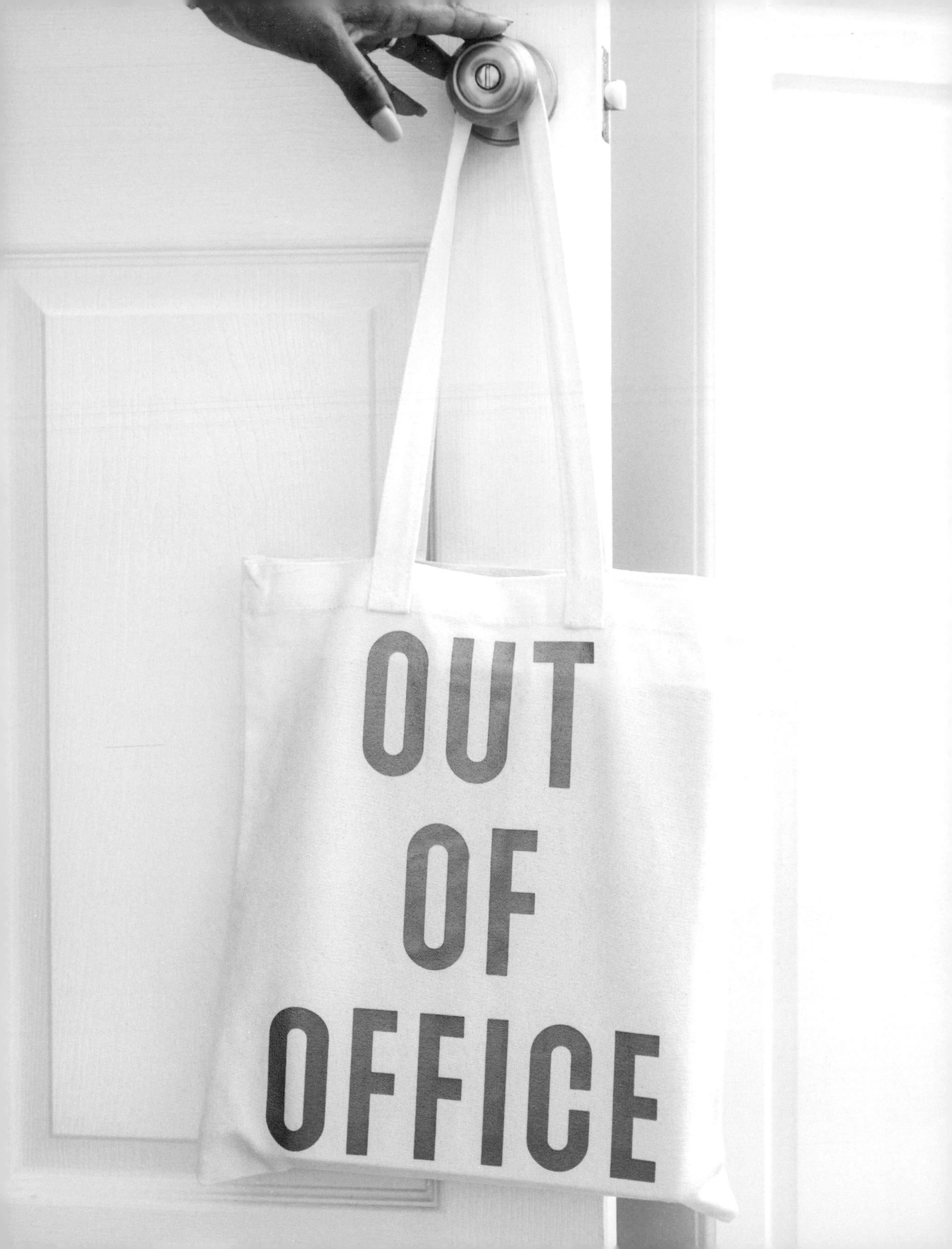
OUT
OF
OFFICE

CONCLUSION

I hope this book has shown you all the ways your work life can be just as beautiful as your home life. The tools I've shared will bring peace and productivity to your workday. They may not be easy to implement overnight, but if you make a commitment to staying organized, you will find yourself feeling more centered and focused over time.

Any time you find yourself tempted to rush through a task—or even your whole day— remember: Feeling frantic is no way to live. You deserve to feel joy and calm, and if you create habits and routines, you will improve your overall mood and attitude toward work. Then you can bring that good mood back home with you at the end of the day.

Before you close this book, stand up. Stretch your arms above your head and take a deep breath. Tell yourself and the universe that you are divorcing stress and returning chaos to the sender. Then write down your top three takeaways from this book and implement them over the next 3 days. Start small and then stay committed to the path ahead. Doing so will give you the motivation you need to get the ball rolling toward becoming more beautifully organized at work.

ACKNOWLEDGMENTS

I can share my passion for the art of organization because I have a beautiful village that supports and inspires me daily.

Thanks to God for giving me my life experiences, both good and bad, because they have helped me become the person I am today and have inspired me to write this book. I also thank God for placing Mike Boyd as my husband. His never-ending support and patience during the writing of this book kept me going. To my parents, I owe you the world for being such great role models for me, both at work and home.

To my Blue Star Press family, we did it! I could not have done this book without you. A special thanks to the editorial director of this book, Lindsay Wilkes-Edrington, for being my rock on this journey. If she did not drink before she met me, I am sure she does now. Peter Licalzi, thanks for always being so supportive and uplifting during the struggle days. A big thank you as well to Camden Hendricks, Brenna Licalzi, and Clare Whitehead, the best behind-the-scenes powerhouse a girl could have.

To Katie Lybrand of Katie Charlotte Photography, you made this book come to life with your beautiful photography. Thanks for the fun photoshoots and laughs. Chris Ramirez, thanks for designing the beautiful pages of this book. To my amazing "At Home With Nikki" team, Jennifer Nielson, Hazel Tiongson, Kate Sonza, Angela Beatty, Olivia Rodd, and Mary Baliton, you complete me! Thanks for all that you do every day to make my life easier. Finally, to all of my YouTube friends, thanks for your years of support and love. You always lift me up, and you are the inspiration behind all that I do!

INDEX